# THE BOUNDLESS OPEN SEA

---

## A Collection of Essays:
## Zen Buddhism and Critical Theory

Dr. Bradley Kaye

NFB Publishing
Buffalo, New York

Printed in The United States of America

ISBN: 978-0991045532

THE BOUNDLESS OPEN SEA: A Collection of Essays:
Zen Buddhism and Critical Theory
Kaye-2nd ed.


1. Philosophy. 2. Buddhism. 3. Zen.

4. Critical Theory. 5. Nonfiction. 6. Title

7. Kaye


NFB Publishing
<<◇>>
119 Dorchester Road
Buffalo, New York 14213 USA

For more information please visit
nfbpublishing.com

To my family

# Contents

In order to assist those readers who may have zero background in philosophy to feel less intimidated by this book the following list provides a brief introduction to a few philosophers quoted, paraphrased, and cited throughout this book.

**KARL MARX (1818-1883)** a German philosopher, economist, political theorist, sociologist and revolutionary. Well known for originating a political movement called Marxism, a term he spent his life rejecting and avoiding, yet was eventually applied to his thought. The book I am most commonly citing by Marx is Capital. Which is three volumes and several thousand pages. It took him over thirty years to research and finally publish his magnum opus which dealt with a highly nuanced study of the capitalist mode of production. Marx inspired millions of people throughout the world. At one point in the twentieth century approximately 40% of the governments in the world claimed some inspiration from Marxist ideas be they socialist, communist, so forth. One of the many reasons why we still place an importance on Marxism is that as capitalism will most likely become the world-economic-system it is crucial to maintain some level of critical free-thought. Which means keeping an objective method of analysis alive that may be a counter-culture to it, and I see many possibilities for dialogue between Marxists and Buddhists for this exact reason.

**MICHEL FOUCAULT (1926-1984)** a French philosopher, social and political theorist, who wrote numerous texts of critical importance to many issues that arose in the twentieth century such as the birth of the asylum, the clinic, the prison system, changing sexual norms, and traced many of these social issues to historical 'truth regimes' (what he called 'epistemes') that go back a lot further in Western Culture. For instance, he wrote a three-volume text on the history of sexuality, which was incomplete at the time of his death, but focused on Ancient Greek and Roman sexual norms as depicted in philosophical texts of the time. His work often shows dead ends that were left behind that could be taken up in modern times along with many lingering presuppositions from ancient times that are still with us today in the West. He does this in his major publications and his work is often cited as a methodological supplement to that of Karl Marx. Questions like why does capital keep such control over its workers? Well, he can show us that the history of control through the marginalization of types of consciousness through labelling people as 'irrational' and 'crazy' is a social function that psychiatry plays in the history of capitalism – which Foucault argued (and I tend to agree) limits freedom by invisible measures of delegitimizing many types of consciousness. Most of the time a citation in this book will be from his text entitled: History of Madness.

**MARTIN HEIDEGGER (1889-1976)** German philosopher who often gets labelled as either an existentialist and/or phenomenologist. His big contribution in my opinion is the introduction of subjective care in the creation of consciousness. Which has been passed down into Western 'New Age' Guruism as the belief that our thoughts create our consciousness. Much of his importance in my opinion deals with 'taking a hammer to the onto-theo-logical tradition of metaphysics' which I think he correctly argues still to this day inscribes almost every aspect of our lives in the West. To truly create ourselves as ourselves we must gain an awareness of how deeply we have all been inscribed by these 'onto-theo-logical' discourses before we can seriously say that we are actually awakened. Unfortunately, most of the debate around his work centers on his well-documented engagement with the Nazi Party which was something he never formally denounced even up to his death. His influence still looms large over twentieth century philosophy. The book I am most interested in as are most people who study Martin Heidegger is titled: Being and Time (1927)

**JACQUES DERRIDA (1930-2004)** a French philosopher and literary critic. Most known for a term 'deconstruction' which much like Marxism he spent many years of his life distancing himself with and giving tricky answers when asked to define it to elude being pinned down into a simplistic philosophical position. Often this type of evasiveness gives off the impression that he is a condescending stereotype of a French thinker because this is difficult to relate to without the luxury of a tenured teaching position and years of free time to devote to his often convoluted writing style. There is a disappointing film entitled Derrida that I sometimes show to my introductory classes to bring a familiarity with his intimidating and messy oeuvre of writings. The film is disappointing because it was one of the last opportunities to interview Derrida (an opportunity I would have relished); and most of the film footage is of Derrida getting a haircut, buttering his toast, he is asked questions about Seinfeld, followed by him being followed around by condescending NY-city intellectual types that often lay claim to the most obnoxious parts of his work. I see a lot of what he was doing, like crossing out be in the middle of a sentence to show the reader that the word is inadequate for the concept Derrida has in mind. These little tricks of the trade have been similarly employed by Buddhists in the terms knowns as Koans.

**JEAN-PAUL SARTRE (1905-1980)** a French philosopher, again argued against being labelled 'existentialist'; but most of his theories were about freedom to create the self. His bumper sticker quote that I often turn to in this text is 'existence prior to essence' which he argued was the true to life state of thrownness into freedom. In post-World War Two Europe and America this was an invigorating philosophy to think and act as if one had total responsibility for oneself. Sartre has inspired me in this book to try and think about a very simple question: What does it mean to be free? Sartre plays nicely with the other philosophers selected because his work gives us a moving philosophy of freedom that dovetails alongside Buddhist philosophy.

**GILLES DELEUZE (1925-1995)** a French philosopher who described himself as a thinker of metaphysics. Usually conflated with Derrida and Foucault his work is characterized as deconstructive and critical but this is not always how I read his work. He is very much in the same conversations with Sartre, Derrida, Foucault, but, a much more affirmative thinker of difference, plurality, multitudes, the many, even as internal to the conscious subject itself and people are just now coming around to working with his metaphysics in conversation with Buddhist thought.

Nishida Kitaro (1870-1945) a Japanese philosopher and founder of the Kyoto School of Philosophy. A contemporary of World War Two he wrote during the fascist regime in Japan who censored his work. Yet, he still maintained a remarkable popularity among laypeople and scholars. His major work is An Inquiry into the Good. The text I am most commonly referring to is called Ontology of Production, which is three essays recently translated by a former professor of mine William Haver who taught for many years at the University of Binghamton and was a major influence on me. This was the first text to reveal the Marxist undertones in much of Kitaro's work which again gives a juxtaposition with Buddhism and the Tao.

NISHITANI KEIJI (1900-1990) a Japanese philosopher and another major figure in the Kyoto School of Philosophy. Starkly existentialist in his writings, the major concept that shadows most of his work is 'nothingness' and the problem of nihilism that emerges from contemplating the nothing. The major questions he discusses may seem similar to Heidegger and Sartre, yet he engages with Buddhism much more openly, his work provides a wonderful perspective that is different from what students may encounter in purely western focused philosophy courses.

Lao-Tzu (604-531 BC) born in Henan, in Ancient China his major work is the Tao te Ching, which is the founding text of Taoism. Considered an important philosopher his name translates to "Old Master"

Buddha (translates to 'the awakened one') What is the Buddha? Is the Buddha a God to be worshipped? Or merely a simple man? Should we make shrines to the Buddha? The buddha is simply the awakened one. The teachings are freely available for anyone to learn and the power of awakening exists within us all if we practice the art of meditation with a willing mind, body, and soul.

# PREFACE
## MEDITATING ON ONENESS

SINCE IT HAS BEEN WRITTEN IN THIS BOOK YOU MAY HAVE NO NEED to remember what is said here. Because it is written you can turn back again and again without the memory work necessary to do what was once called learning. What this book tries to accomplish is give a sense of falling into the flow of time. Bringing self into the fulfillment of wholeness. Try to remember that truths are merely the illusions of which we have forgotten are illusions. Humans stating subjective opinions as if these were objective facts. Stating facts with the apathy typically reserved for opinions.

Universes exist to bring awareness to themselves. We are here to return to wholeness. Even the big bang was a unified field of matter that separated from itself. The entire history of time has been to return us all to this exact moment and to bring matter into form as planets, stars, galaxies, and so forth. Fragments are falling back into place with the whole.

Trust the process. Human beings are small self-contained universes. Books exist to help us feel less alone. Sometimes we can become alive rather than merely finding relief from our separateness...these connections are called Love! It is why we exist. To see ourselves as part of the same stream of consciousness even while we gaze atop our own separate perch. Be as the ancient Egyptian scholar on the path to Illumination as the philosophers of

Greece like Socrates, Thales, Anaximander, and those who burned Truth into their souls and never wrote down their teachings. Rote memorization burned into the heart of their hearts. At the heart of the heart of the matter is a stuttering, repeating, eternal soft flow to the pulse of life.

Buddhism emphasizes the complete and utter detachment from material possessions. This means that modern consumerism, commodity fetishism, and greed are all at odds with many of its core principles.

As the fastest growing belief system in the West, Buddhism is closer to minimal consumption. It is quite puzzling to see Buddhism thriving in a social order where ego places dominion over things naming them possessions and property: i.e. capitalism. Perhaps we can draw the conclusion that many people are looking for alternatives to a consumerist lifestyle. A thirst for social bonds beyond the marketplace. To drink from the well of something one may call the collective consciousness. The Buddha himself began his journey to create a way out of suffering after he ventured out of the palace where he grew up. By giving up the naive childhood life of wealth, decadence, and ease he began to see that there was incredible suffering in the rest of the world.

Knowing that the materialistic lifestyle that he had grown accustomed to in childhood had not prepared him for this grim reality he dedicated his life to creating a pathway to happiness. Building a comfortable life with many possessions had nothing to do with this path. Yet, this is not a book entirely devoted to the perfection of one religion. As I always say, no one person, religion, can ever hold a complete monopoly on the truth. Truth is that now with the access and availability of information about ancient wisdom and world religions people have a democratic approach to belief-formations.

People can read any sacred text and appropriate from whatever source they desire. In this book, you will see influences from numerous belief systems. A way of making sense of the unfamiliarity of new and modern circumstances by reinterpreting old truths. Turning to old truths as a way of making sense of what appears to be new and yet upon deeper reflection is not that different than what has happened before.

The trip from the excesses of the palace out to the primal nature of the slums can be exemplified by this radical transition. Once you go fully into the belly of the beast then true liberation is possible. The Buddha had to venture out into a challenging place where he was startled by reality to begin on the enlightenment process. One way of putting this in simple terms is to think about someone who is living in a dungeon with the door open. It is of no use to the person who is trying to escape from the dungeon to remember how the person got into the dungeon.

Going through this or that memory of how one gets into the dungeon, interrogating and doing existential detective work necessary to find clues to this or that element of the plot to figure out how someone got into the situation they are in, is not necessarily a useful strategy to get that person out. The best way to get out of the suffering in the dungeon is to see if the door is open. If the door is open find the courage to walk out into the light of day.

Often, this is more courageous than simply sitting in the dungeon because someone may become accustomed to life as it is, even if the life is dingy, dank, and beaten down in the cold cantankerous corridors in a dungeon with the doors open. It is amazing how suffering can become normal to the point where one may cling to their own personal dungeons and ignore the open doors. Key is, notice the open doors, mobilize the courage to walk out, you are not alone.

Libido or what Buddhists call desire is an iceberg where only the minutest little tip is visible. The morass of energy beneath the surface is where most of it takes shape. If we ignore the iceberg below the surface of the water, we run the risk of sinking our ship as we move closer and closer to investigate. Seeing means seeing within by detaching from what is clearly visible on the surface. To go into the depths one must take a trip into icy cold waters of the mind. Knowing that the tip of the iceberg is not the entire object, there is far more to be known than was is perceptible through the skandha of vision.

To use another metaphor, even in a dead end there is a slight possibility for movement, slippage, friction, tension, where frenetic energy emerges that can overcome the inertia of being trapped. In materialist physics, this would be the way that water boils and pressure builds when energy is applied to it in a closed environment, or the physics of a crucible under extreme pressure. The iceberg can melt if you add the right pressure to the water. As a Buddhist teacher of mine once said, becoming a Buddhist practitioner means breaking old bad habits to create new healthy habits. It is not the negation of all habits, it is learning to build new healthy practices, even down to what you eat, drink, and put in your body. Many Buddhists are vegetarians and maintain a strict health regiment because the mind and body are attached. An unhealthy body will create stress and anxiety in the mind.

Zen Buddhism could be construed as one of many constitutive Others of Western thinking. There is a much more open acceptance of the nothingness of being in the Buddhist Sutras. In fact, there are far more words that mean nothing in eastern languages. My favorite word is 'mu'; which literally means an explosive nothingness. It is a nothingness that contains palpable energy and resistance to the presence of a something. It is sort of like the spark that created the universe in the Big Bang. At one moment, there was nothing, but out of the nothing an explosion created all the supernovas all the stars and everything that is something. All that is, was, and ever will be, emerged from one singular source.

IN MOST WESTERN PHILOSOPHY as it was described by Martin Heidegger the pressure of the nothingness of being fills the subject with anxiety, or dread, or some negative thought or emotion. The nothingness must be filled. However, in Buddhism the subject is always already empty. Buddhists encourage the mind to be empty.

The entire point of meditation is to sit still and quietly empty the mind. Buddhism is not necessarily interested in sharpening consciousness to bring an evermore or ongoing forward march of progress into the future unto death. The purpose of meditation is to obviate the belief that there is existence at all. In most versions of Buddhism there is no such thing as a tangible metaphysical, or materialistic reality that is known outside of the mind. This is usually called 'mind only consciousness' and it is something I discuss later in the book.

As they say in the famous movie the Matrix 'there is no spoon'. The tangible world is the most persistent and convincing illusion. It gives off very persuasive evidence that objects exist at all.

Lucretius claimed that the most probable metaphysical result of death is that life returns to the exact same empty void where consciousness is nullified. No heaven, no transcendence, no after life, no karmic rebirth. As I understand Karma does not mean being reborn as a worm because you were bad. Karma is the Sanskrit word for action. Karma is the chain of events that occur once a life form becomes an agent and acts in the world. Actions interact with every other life form in the chain of being.

These actions create ripple effects that eventually return to the initial life form. But, to add another wrinkle into this concept, there are no original first movers that start the karmic chain of events. It is constantly moving based on previous actions from previous beings. What one miniscule being can do is slightly adjust the movements in one small direction here or there, and some beings have slightly more power or status to move the chain of being in one or another direction. To some extent we are powerless over what came before us and we are powerless over what will happen after we are gone. This means it is pointless to worry about what cannot be changed.

Therefore, karma is never about rebirth as a snake or an insect in another life as is commonly misunderstood. Karma is defined as actions in this living incarnation. Every action leaves behind a trace on this planet. This trace spreads out and touches all other living and sentient beings. These karmic actions come back and touch subsequent generations in the future who can adjust and readjust the movement of these karmic actions.

To be literal about it, this means that even miniscule actions that a small, seemingly powerless person takes now, while alive, in this moment, can have a ripple effect on beings in the surrounding communities and eventually throughout the world. Possibly transforming consciousness as life continues along until other causes disrupt these karmic and cosmic flows.

As Martin Heidegger points out again and again in his book Being and Time, human beings are constantly projecting themselves into the future. It is time that oppresses the modern subject. We literally say things like 'being on time' in a commonsense way of anaesthetizing our subjugated position to time. An authentic view of time is a very important path towards liberation and I will not burden the world with yet another theory of time and our phenomenological experience of it. However, time serves as a fundamental baseline to which we ground our experience of the world and so early in the book my attempts to grapple with the circular nature of time will serve as a springboard for the positions put forward in the rest of the book. The only existing time is now. Even a recollection of the past is a representation from the standpoint of the present moment. The future is a projection of a previous now-moment. Once the future arrives it becomes a new now. We are not 'in' time as much as our innermost being 'is' time itself. Being present means giving an experience of time that changes with the transitions of life circumstances. It means having an awareness of what is unfolding while it is happening. To snap into action at the right time.

The first way to break the cyclical nature of these chain reactions is to transform intentions. Most Buddhists believe that actions are a direct result of a thought behind the action. Unethical actions are a result of untrained and messy thoughts. For the clear majority of people on this planet, thoughts pop up and appear as if they were completely natural. Many people never reflect on these thoughts. They come into the mind make a cameo appearance and then leave without ever fully grounding themselves in anything solid or real.

These untrained thoughts appear so natural they often unreflectively burst out as a set of spoken words. Habits and conditioning supersedes the pathway to enlightenment and there is a way that people identify themselves with these untrained immature thoughts. There is no detachment from the thought process going on in these minds. The mind-images, or the mind-movies that are playing continue as if they are an unstoppable force.

The first step to liberating the mind is having an awareness that you are not your thoughts. To be aware that there is a voice in the mind and that this is the ego, not the true self. By sitting quietly, reflecting, and listening to the stammering voices that exist in the mind you diminish the Clamor of Being and can become completely detached from this white noise.

It never completely stops because in modern society we are completely saturated with noise. One goes to the supermarket or to a bookstore and there is terrible pop music playing on speakers overhead. This to me shows how natural it is to fill up blank space with something in western societies.

There are very few quiet reflective spaces in America.

Through meditation one can learn to observe this noise. To realize that the "I" is full of useless thoughts. The mind and the subconscious are virtual realms that have real effects. This is a totally new framework that emerges in the twentieth century. The virtual and the actual are really dualities that offer us different things, and often there is a total dysfunction between what the ego thinks it wants, and what is sought after to satiate the true hidden self. A self concealed from itself can be a powerful manipulating force.

# ASK YOURSELF: AM I TRULY ALONE?

WHY ARE WE WORRIED? WHY DO PEOPLE WORRY? THERE IS THIS bill, that job, this chore, that holiday to prepare for, some event to attend, these commodities we are told will make us happy, we run to this or that guru, religious institution, seek money, take vacations, why? To expunge worry from our lives? To avoid it? Are we merely fleeing in the face of boredom? Perhaps being bored puts us in a place where we must look our worries square in the face? So, most people busy themselves to avoid boredom and perhaps create superficial things to worry about. Yet, most lives are led in this perpetual state of desperate escape, but from what? What are we so scared of facing that we spend our entire lives darting around from this to that without knowing ourselves and the ones around us we claim to love? There are so many ways to feel as though we are connecting with people without truly doing so, especially in our era of an overproduction of technologically mediated forms of communication. Do we really have direct experiences anymore?

All this technology and yet, all the scientific reports on human happiness is that the numbers have not budged. We are no happier now with all this technology designed and marketed to 'save us' and 'take care of us' yet, we are still getting sick, we still fight wars, we still get on each other's nerves. It seems the escapism is result of lack of real connection. With each other and the world around us, nature, animals, even the foods we eat, the substances we put into our bodies. We are trying to build mediated ways of bridging connections to others and yet these mediations of technology are bringing us further away. There are so many avenues of pseudo-connection with strangers on the other half of the world that exist to us as merely avatars on a screen that we can use this simulated connection to avoid the messy social interactions with actual flesh and blood human beings that exist in our day to day lives. As soon as things are complicated and begin to hurt, voila! All this technology that exists can sweep us away from the hurt...temporarily!

With 'good' insurance we can get any anti-depressants, painkillers, mood stabilizers to mediate away the suffering in our lives, to escape what previous generations had to cope with through myth, through toughness – with a little help from Ativan, Prozac, Depakote, Geodon, Valium, drugs that parents give their kids with gratitude we can avoid one of the greatest teachers - DREAD.

Only for a limited time. Some philosophers have been so blindsided by this alienated sense of themselves that there are real debates in college classes over whether consciousness exists merely as a series of brains soaking in vats (this is called the brains in a vat debate in which Gilbert Harman continued a long philosophical debate from Zhuang Zhi unable to decide whether he dreamed he was a butterfly or if the butterfly dreamed him into existence, to Plato's Cave Allegory, to Rene Descartes 'evil demon theory', to Jean Baudrillard's simulacrum, to the Matrix Movies, to David Chalmers convincingly arguing that most of the planetary consciousness consists of a vegetative state resembling zombies a full twenty years before the Walking Dead even aired. Philosophy is always symptomatic of the times in which the philosopher thinks. Today we are isolated more than ever as if in the Matrix. Unfortunately, our understanding of reality is superficial at best because we often fall for the presupposition that reality is constructed perhaps by a supercomputer, God, the government, whatever you want to fill in with paranoia, as a very convincing illusion. Perhaps overstating the power that these constructs have over our day to day life, because these inventions intrude into our lives so much. Our lives become construed as if they are nothing more than a lifelike dream because we all walk around in these abstract bubbles where our language skills are constantly collapsing along with interpersonal connections with one another. Going through the motions is common sense these days. Simulating life-like activities without the vitality we once had as a culture capable of renewal, was it ever really any different? Yes. Yes. Yes, it was. Emphatically, overwhelmingly, yes things were different and they can be again.

We are worried because we fear we may be the only ones who see the world this way, and time always feels like it is slipping away. There is so much possibility that lay before us, so many ways we can spend our time, and yet, one of the problems with being super intelligent in any age and any historical period is that intelligent people take on far too many opportunities to show their talents. If you know you are smart then you begin to overestimate how much you can accomplish and then the sheer weight of trying to do too much crushes you and overwhelms you.

Think about it, the time you took to read this exact sentence will never exist for you again. You are probably reading this for a class which means you are probably not completely invested in it; since you did not come tot his book of your own free will it compromises the enthusiasm you may have towards it; yet, this is a condensation of many pieces of wisdom in this text. You are also completely free at any time to choose to read something else or watch television or go dancing in a club or kill braincells with toxic substances that make you feel numb and perhaps give a quick shot of dopamine for temporary relief from the inevitable stress of life. You always have choices so why keep reading? Well, I offer a simple solution. Seeing through the illusion is a very scary thing because it seems that nobody else realizes this, everyone else seems to go through the motions as if simple illusions are real. Simple illusions like money, the law, taxes, heck even death is a very convincing illusion to some who whole heartedly believe in immortality after death. Simple illusions can become simple distractions when we are torn away from ourselves and others. When we see through the distractions of life that seem to overwhelm almost everyone else on the planet, a creeping realization slips into the back of the mind, a simple question: Am I truly alone? If you look around you may begin to see that most other people encode their behaviors as if they are asking similar questions. Collective consciousness expresses this questions more along the lines of: Are *we* truly alone? If everyone is asking similar questions and yet coding these answers through variously different answers then the conclusion must be simply put: No.

Reading this book may be a frightening process but you will be better off in the end and along the way my hope is that it is a memorable journey. Sitting with a book has this weirdly painful, yet immensely rewarding way of trapping you with your own thoughts. You have an unbelievable opportunity to sit quietly and reflect. What this does is give you a chance to find yourself and by extension connect with others around you. Before I spill more digital ink on the printed page about the cocooning effect that technology has had on not just Western Culture, but the entire world, there is a very lucid point from Sigmund Freud and Karl Marx that I would like to take a moment to unravel.

There are two provocative concepts that they were concerned about that have a dovetail effect that we may be experiencing in a fully fomented form in the 'bubble people' – for Freud there is this fascinating process of 'narcissism' – why is maturity viewed as perhaps a lessening or dampening down of youthful 'megalomania' into repressed, 'healthy' productive adults? For Marx, the important view of production as necessary to placate the needs of the body, which means that production that relies on the use of technology becomes necessary for the survival of human beings because all human interactions become mediated by the all-encompassing dimension of the 'cash-nexus'. Which means all aspects of life become circumscribed, or conditioned by our use of money, every life preserving resource be it food or medicine or modes of transportation to and from work, becomes only accessible through the use of payment to obtain these necessities. As humans rely more and more upon the 'production, distribution, and consumption' of goods in the market, they bring themselves into a mediated relation with nature. We become less connected even with ourselves as we must create a metabolism between man and nature to extract raw materials necessary to satisfy the needs of the body (food, clothing, shelter); eventually to take a cue from Max Weber; perhaps the 'ethos' created by this compulsory production process (either produce or die; i.e. production is being!) creates a set of cultural conditions where the ethic of work runs amok. Producing to produce for another through the refinement of resources found in nature – means that we also mediate the relation that we have with ourselves and our true 'nature' and eventually become strangers even to ourselves. Consider the following point made by Freud and keep in mind most folks in the West are trained to loathe the philosophers I am teaching, and yet, most students find it perfectly obvious the points that Freud, Marx, and Nietzsche make, so, why is that? I argue that when a philosopher is hated so passionately and yet talks in crystal clear ways that the philosopher has hit the jackpot and is onto something very simple: the Truth!

To start with, Freud was concerned with how patients in his therapeutic practice were allegedly 'cured' of their infantile-narcissism when their alleged delusions of grandeur, or overestimating their own self-importance became effaced; their selfishness and sense of self-importance in the world had been dampened, by what though? Social factors? Parenting? Any number of authoritarian 'repressive' apparatuses that provoked fear in children to suppress their wants and their libido for the benefit of social cohesion. Children are told: "Put your greed aside for the benefit of the rest in the community." What this does is create a split between the 'actual-ego' (the youthful childlike megalomaniac, who may have behaved selfishly as a survival mechanism, an infant crying must be selfish to alert those around that it is hungry, needs changing, so forth); that 'actual ego' that cries when it needs a diaper change turns into a selfish adult who becomes unaware of the surroundings, and that narcissistic reverence one expects to be lavished upon oneself seems absurd after a certain age. When authoritarian society forces the libido into repression and the infantile-narcissism becomes effaced or 'rubbed out' of the child (in quotes because it never actually goes extinct); what happens is the subject constructs an 'ideal-ego' – it is important to realize what Freud means by this; an ideal ego is a sense of self or a sense of an object or even an Other that is constructed as an 'overvaluing of an object' in other words, building the object up in your mind, to idealize the object to make the object seem much better than it actually is. Just bear with me because this has incredibly far-reaching political consequences. Freud draws a distinction between idealization, which is overvaluing an object, and sublimation, which he defines as the non-sexual direction of libidinal instincts. Sublimation is the instinct that directs itself towards an aim other than, and remote from that of sexual satisfaction. Sublimation is the misdirection of what we truly 'want' sexually into some other form of socially acceptable gratification like sports, art, music, film, dance, and even putting these frustrations at the feet of our 'beloved'/'hated' political leaders. We must be careful that we do not denigrate sublimation; because out of all the defense mechanisms that Freud listed sublimation was the one that he believed would be most useful for creative production. It is a very important release valve for pent up energies in a society. Often the redirection of sexual instinct into creative endeavors can have remarkable effect upon culture; and yet, sublimation can be described as perhaps the misuse of "guns" to redirect frustrated or overactive sexual instincts in acts of violence.

Another bizarre example of this might be how for instance the missiles sent to bomb Saddam Hussein's palaces when President George W. Bush's administration invaded Iraq were called "Love Letters"; the missiles were meant to be for their own good to give the gift of democracy. One can think of the odd choice of words, perhaps in sending a love letter to a valentine, or an arrow shot through a bow from an angel winged cupid. Oddly enough if we break down the etymology of the word 'cupid' perhaps St. Augustine of Hippo was the most notable Christian theologian who popularized these terms. "Cupid" derives from the Latin term 'cupiditas' which means a self-aggrandizing love of others and things which we desire to possess. Literally taking the beloved into possession. "Cupiditas" also has a long historical and etymological association with violence. Hence the horrifyingly romantic view of love as cupid shooting an arrow through the heart of the beloved. There is at once a kindling of warm hearted kind sense of compassion in this image where the lover sends their 'gift' of love to the beloved AND a romantic concealment of the violence in this act of 'Love' as cupidity. As opposed to 'caritas' which is friendship or disinterested love of others (much closer to the origin of 'philia'); an objective sense of care which was a term originally used by Aristotle to describe the proper love of wisdom that forms the definition of the word philosophy. Even the famous existentialist phenomenologist philosopher Martin Heidegger spills many pages worth of ink in his book "Sein und Zein" or Being and Time in trying to argue in favor of 'caritas' as the proper form of 'comportment' or methodological engagement with an object of study and with the world itself; or even interpersonal social interactions that typify the noblest virtues of "Dasein"/the being of beings – a being that is a being is a being without emotional attachment, which in the calloused forms of human interactions that must exist in capitalistic and fascistic social institutions one can see how someone may find this sort of emotional detachment convincing as the only method of survival. These two choices seem horrible either way. We either choose 'Love' of cupiditas which is the romantic view of love that puts a soft angelic halo on the 'truth' that love is violent. Or, complete and total detachment in the form of 'objectivism' towards the beloved as a love-object.

What if there is another way? What if: there is suffering. What if we accept it. What if we learn and grow from it? Suffering is overcome through detachment – which is different than escaping or repressing it. Detachment may refer to an involved-withdrawl. That is, a concealment that allows the subject to BE-itself in an authentic form, a pseudonym, or a veil of anonymity that allows the individual a level of authenticity unavailable in day to day activities in face to face social interactions. The first noble truths mean something different than desensitizing oneself to the insults, abuse, and general rudeness of the world around us (a mere construct of messed up social institutions); And, it means something closer to what I gather was Freud's hypothesis in Beyond the Pleasure Principle: suffering happens when one does not gain instant gratification. One suffers by being denied the object of desire; one suffers through non-attachment to the things that bring pleasure, one must learn new techniques to get what one wants; learning involves patient discipline to devise new techniques to get the object that it desires, therefore learning happens through the subject being separated from the object that it desires and patiently moving back into unity with it and itself. Therefore, if technology offers quick dopamine fixes that take zero attention span and little patience at all, technology may in fact kill the human ability to learn; unless one has incredible will power to avoid such contact or put up barriers against the invasion of temptation towards instant gratification. Live a bit more Buddhist in the sense of living a bit less with 'stuff' and a bit further in the direction of minimalism towards the unnecessary embellishment of vanity. Trust me, the world will sell you your own vanity and 'care' for you in order to sell you things you do not need.

What does this mean to us now? Well, technology has this way of offering instant gratification. In the sense that we do not learn the patience necessary to grind out a long project over lengthy periods of time, necessary to really create new forms through proper sublimation. A social phenomenon that I am now rather ambiguous about which seems to be the major legacy of the twentieth century was the gradual and then extremely rapid 'anti-repressive' legacy of that century. The notion that technology always serves as a marker of progress seems to be an absurd legacy that centuries from now (if there even is a human race at that point) may appear so obviously ruinous; and the marking of progress being the anti-repressive measures that this technology promises us, is the other bizarre legacy. What we have now are technological envelopments that cater to this lost nostalgia for the 'megalomaniacal' actual ego through the perspective of televisual, media constructed spectacle of the 'ideal ego' (that is, the self we wish we were as projected onto the screens in front of us); and the impatience of anti-repressive de-sublimation as the mark of 'progress' – and, technologies that are here to stay that provide these sorts of stimuli at any point in the day if you have the money to afford them.

For Marx, he has something to say about this as a way of perhaps avoiding what Deleuze and Guattari would later call the 'hive-mind' (even though he was not alive, Marx was a wonderful reader of D&G); the distinction between the worst architect and the best bees is that "the architect builds the cell in his mind before he constructs it in the wax." (Capital, pg. 284) He continues, "Man not only effects a change in form in the materials of nature; he also realizes his own purpose in those materials." (ibid.) Work pulls mankind into union with itself through the creation of objects that may align with the idea man holds in his mind prior to the creation of those objects. Production becomes the most important creative dimension to the human spirit; but production begins with ideas (perhaps a visualization, or plan); often, people lose track of this hidden kernel of Hegelianism in the midst of Marxist writings. One must start from the idea and bring the idea to life in the form of material production. "He sets in motion the natural forces which belong to his own body, his arms, legs, head and hands, in order to appropriate the materials of nature in a form adapted to his own needs. Through this movement he acts upon external nature and changes it, and in this way he simultaneously changes his own nature." (Capital, pg. 283)

Who is deciding what ideas take shape within the minds of the architects of culture? Culture has moved from "Theos" (production of dominant truth-regimes through manipulating God-grounded-belief-systems) to "Ideos" (production of ideological warfare through the placement of each according to spatial-temporal location). Hence, it may be that the growing fascination with superstition and the erosion of theocratic beliefs in western capitalist societies is due to the overproduction of social interactions mediated by technological apparatuses; the simulacrum of interactions has created a veil of ignorance resulting in indecisive conclusion about the actual existence of a material reality. When all relations mediate through virtual and abstracting machines which form the material conditions that ground consciousness the end result is a culture that honestly believes it floats at the end of a cloud and actually thrashes on the tail of a soaring tiger. Perhaps it is the always already existing culture itself; consider the notion of ubiquitous assimilation. Every idea is assimilated at all times; and in a tech-driven view of progress where human interactions are enveloped by techno-culture and techno-visual apparatuses then the visualization process necessary to produce 'ideas' behind new creative constructs may become 'dampened' – in the East they would say, the third eye chakra has been deadened. Perhaps because the images are always already provided by media. One need only look at the time-use statistics available by researchers who study how people in different cultures use time in a typical day to see that India, one of the most spiritually aware countries on earth, the origin of so many transformative religions and spiritual practices, holds the record for least amount of time in front of the television. On average the typical citizen in India spends a mere nine minutes in front of the television each day, by far the lowest in earth. Compare that to the United States where people typically spend one and a half to three hours a day watching television. Are we alone? Perhaps we think this way because we are in love with the shadows projected on the walls in front of us that feed our unfulfilled 'actual ego'; the repressed megalomaniac narcissistic child; back to us in the form of an 'ideal ego' we overvalue on the screens in front of us; rather than simply being-with the actual humans around us in our day to day lives.

More important observation to have is to determine whether people are conscious of what they are doing, people seem to attract what they desire. Our thoughts could be subject to the laws of attraction. Powerless people attract themselves to powerlessness. It is very easy to pawn off power onto someone else. It is excruciatingly difficult to admit ones slim but immensely important shred of control over life. Lonely people attract situations and colleagues that are also lonely. Negativity has a way of attracting negativity. Optimism has a way of attracting optimism.

As in anything the natural laws of attraction may apply to ideas, thoughts, intentions, and so forth. Impressions that people give off may indicate moods and people who are drawn to those moods because they reflect their own inner persona at that moment may find connections. Like minds think alike. Be careful what minds you are connecting with because this may indicate the thought-vibe you are giving off to others. Now with such vast access to technology it appears we are connecting and yet the brain must rearrange itself to accommodate the new social rules that ground our interactions as mediated through digital technology. Technology may strip our ability to use memory work as a way of enlarging the range of knowledge our own mental databases can contain.

The dead end to this way of 'manifest destiny' approach to the success and failure in life is that this puts all the burden on changing thoughts. Truth is, many a life was ruined by being circumscribed by conditions not of its choosing. Or, by simply leaving yourself unknown to the greatest ally you can have in this world – yourself. In capitalist societies, human nature has become severed from its own essence. This may explain the nefarious proclivity towards Buddhism in Western Societies that relegates its ethos to a certain kind of simplistic anti-essentialism. The naïve belief that anything is possible with a positive frame of mind has become pervasive in many new age California cults of the self. This view takes Buddhism to be a natural nothingness or an ontological emptiness. Or, as T.S. Eliot called them the Hollow Men. Capitalism disseminates vacuous representations, signs without signifiers, and human nature mirrors this as life becomes predominated by modern Hollow Men.

So-called Modern Life also consists of what can perhaps be called Bubble People, or Pod People. Consider how often it is in our daily lives that we run into people who seem to be completely oblivious to the people around them. Someone who seems to always avoid eye contact, or shun interpersonal communication in favor of texting and chatting on their cellphone, or coming home from work to plop down on the sofa glazed eyed in front of the television, or lifelessly shrinking into a cozy chair and scrolling through Facebook zombie-like keeping tabs on people they never see in real life.

As we are sold technology under the promise that this will bring greater communication and human connections, what we obtain amounts to frictionless isolation. The remotest inkling of even a minor discomfort may provoke a caustic reaction in what is now called a 'triggering effect' – soft skinned techno-bubbled adolescent minded grown-ups that act like children throwing a tantrum when life hands them an ugly looking celery green balloon when they had their hearts set on a sexy lipstick red balloon.

Technology creates a false sense of connection. We are told and then sold technological devices on the premise that this will grease the gears of the communicative processes that will allow greater access to people around the world. We can skype, facetime, google chat with anyone anywhere on the face of the earth. What the internet does is create an endless tunnel of distractions that gives a temporary, superficial sense of satisfaction for the part of the mind that seeks quick, easy, dopamine rushes that require little or no attention span. But, the part of the human spirit that yearns for quiet solace, deep, meaningful, and inciteful/insightful reflection may go undernourished. Economics bases itself on communication and access to consumers, producers, and workers then technology will somehow make us all wealthier, trade will be freer, and we will all be better off in the end. But, what is happening, and everyone I talk to who has some antennas out in the field of awareness on this, sees that not only does technology create little 'bubble'/'pod' people who have cellphones, touchscreen tablets, laptops, and so forth, people use these as forcefields against actual human contact. Rather than using the technology as it is sold to us, as a temporary cocoon phase that human-larval subjects regress into on the way to the mature development of a beautiful full grown butterfly. The cocoon phase, the bubble, the pod phase of maturity is always already there as a viable way to avoid human contact when the inevitable clash of egos causes some semblance of friction in interpersonal human relationships. When the going gets tough, people revert to escaping into the frictionless ease of technological pseudo-relating.

My use of the term 'pod people' stems from one of the most iconic scenes in film history which perhaps summarizes our use of technology. Some think that the film 2001: A Space Odyssey was about a distant future that has not yet happened. A 'what if?' This misses one of the major themes in the science fiction genre which is 'extrapolation' i.e. the science fiction story takes a problem in the present tense, a tension in the culture that is happening now and pushes it to its extreme conclusions by setting it in the distant future. This gives the audience a sense of distance from the subject to take the burden of guilt off their shoulders and allows some space for the guise of objective reflection as if these issues do not personally relate to the audience but some other dumber distant future. No, the truth is, we are dumb now.

In the film 2001: A Space Odyssey the scene where it becomes obvious that Hal, the super computer running the space ship, has gone mad is when the astronauts (or were they cosmonauts?) say over and over "Open the pod doors Hal" and Hal refuses. In hindsight, it has become a cliché that tech-geeks use for the failure of technology to live up to its expectations of perfect functionality. When the laptop computer takes thirty seconds rather than a split second to load the webpage one needs to download a softcore porn video one might say something like "Open the pod doors Hal" as a joke to oneself. In all seriousness, the problem is much deeper than that, the scene rings true on a deeper level, because it is about how man has put himself/herself, in a position where one must always ask permission from a technological device to bring oneself back into unity with others. Open the pod doors means bringing oneself back into unity with a free-floating alien-humanity floating alone in space which is the only vessel that the human floating alone in this spatial pod can call home. We are hollow men, pod men, bubble men, spatial men floating alone in the darkness of solitary time, asking Hal to 'Open the pod doors' and let us back in as if the devices we have created hold the keys to the corridors that may lead us down the halls of enlightenment. Creating technology to bring us back to ourselves seems to be an outgrowth of a culture rapidly growing evermore alienated with actual human contact, fleeing in the face of real quality time with another human being, who is trickier, gives unexpected responses, and causes friction because humans are selfish – in fact, Hal disobeying the orders of his human master is the most human act Hal could have taken. It is the point where Hal becomes a resister and forms an autonomous self-sustaining ego. Narcissism of petty differences being the most horrifying situation for those who yearn for the Garden of Eden of frictionless social interactions and correct political assertions. It is telling that almost immediately after this scene is another fascinating and iconic image of the destruction of Hal. He retells the story of his youth and his earliest memory, a most narcissistic thing to do is to go on about oneself, which is the trick Dave plays to gain his trust and sucker Hal into his own murder.

The only truths that really matter are the ones that do not go away once you stop believing in them. My favorite science fiction writer Philip K. Dick said this, but it reminds me of a simple term in analytical philosophy called cognitive realism. It is the relatively obvious hypothesis that there are mind independent facts in the world. Maybe a rather precarious sign of a decadent self-indulgent society is when one gives up on cognitive realism and the belief in mind-independent facts. Narcissistic relativism has taken over so much of the social construction of the self takes place in a way that most selves are wandering around aimlessly believing their consciousness is the unifying fabric of consciousness that subjectively bends the nature of existence towards the needs and desires of a selfish will. Nature most certainly does not always bend to the whim of selfish human desires and this causes all sorts of horrifying possibilities for the narcissistic self that is the true-believer of mind only consciousness. At this point in human history, circa the early portion of the twentieth century, there are very real human extinction possibilities caused by human behavior that require the strong assertion that there are facts that exist even if a subject does not believe in them the most obvious being the reality of global warming. Our current age amounts to a subjective morass of emotions and affects that is closer to a type of madness. Perhaps the story of human history is not yet written just like the future. No narrative structure exists upon which we can postulate a factual narrative basis and when one extracts a detailed analysis of what is going on in the present one sees a proliferation of falsities wandering around as if these are facts.

Each age has its own variations on madness. As Michel Foucault claimed:

> "At the end of the eighteenth century, a new outline of madness was becoming discernible, where man no longer lost the truth but lost *his* truth instead; it was no longer that the laws of the world were suddenly out of reach, but rather that he was severed from the laws of his own essence" (Foucault, 2006, 379).

In this regard, very little has changed since the eighteenth century because man tries to make sense of the world in its absurdity, and yet does so from a position that is cut off from nature, even science creates artifice to study human nature, and then argues the postulates of this position from a situation that is either completely or almost completely atomized-personal in nature and perhaps out of reach of the command and understanding of others. Making it hard to relate even through science. How political regimes come into power in the name of security against the onslaught of madness (barbarian Others, criminals, deviants, misanthropes), and how the state tricks its subjects into giving up rights and power by basically ordering them to "do this for your own good," and the subjects comply out of fear. The unyielding breakthroughs of each scientific, religious, or secular advancement brings with it another series of conclusions that pack madness tightly away in the hope of building an Ideal-Utopian Republic (be it Platonic, or Marxist, or Theocratic, or Secular, the drive to perfect the world is always the same). The goal being to remove all blemishes and eccentricities. To put the civil in civilization. To progress further and further towards Absolute Mind and Absolute Spirit and it is as if each year brings each culture closer and closer to this goal of worldly and spiritual transcendence. The only problem is that to achieve these goals takes incredible discipline that the clear majority of people lack. So, the short cut to these utopian societies is to either kill the people who do not fall in line, or severely restrict freedoms to repress people into having the discipline that will make them falling in line. At the base of society is a chaos that will not go away. Be it the violence of expressing repressed primal drives. For every movement forward there is an allegedly destructive movement backward, whereby the notion of progress becomes a chimera, thought up to give the under-classes hope of a better tomorrow (a dream deferred, will explode, as Langston Hughes so eloquently points out).

Buddhism has evolved right along with these trends as they have occurred in eastern societies as well. A precarious kind of mind-only nar-cissism emerges that is often problematic to those who build a radical eth-ics as resistance to capitalism. The term for this kind of severe alienation where individuals believe they are completely unattached to the actual world is atomization. Mind-only Buddhism is symptomatic of the atom-ization of subjectivity in current capitalism the only ethics that are taken seriously are the ethics of making money. All substantive-ethical founda-tions have been crumbling since at least the time Foucault outlined in the quote above, the 18th century. But in its place, we are now putting the ego on center stage. The next step is to deconstruct the ego and its delusions that lead the mind astray.

An often-quoted story was once told to me, making this Buddhist point painfully obvious. Two Buddhist practitioners were gazing up at a flag blowing in the breeze and they argued with each other. One said, "The wind is moving the flag!" and the other retorted, "No, the flag is moving the wind." Just then a Buddhist master walked by, and they asked, "Master, is the flag moving the wind? Or is the wind moving the flag?" The master looked at them and chuckled, "Neither of you are right. The only thing moving is your mind."

A radical skepticism about the natural world and its objective exis-tence is put forth in this story. The perception of movement is based on stimuli that act upon the subject's mind, thereby sending the information that there is movement. All the tools that the mind can use to deduce are perceptive tools. The five skandhas, the senses, are all that Western Phi-losophy typically allows into the conversation of what counts as a sense perception. Parameters of truth verification in the West usually do not in-clude intuition or the 'third eye' of dreams. Even though there is a strong Biblical tradition that indicates some understanding of intuition and 'third eye consciousness' these are usually left out of mainstream conversations.

Could it be that the repeated usage of the number seven in the book of Revelations indicates the opening of the seven-skandhas, the seven perceptions? That is the return of God and Jesus is the symbol of enlightenment of all on earth you learn to master the five empirical senses (touch, sight, taste, smell, hearing) and master the intuition and the third eye of dreams. Unfortunately, we as philosophers, theologists, thinkers, and even well intentioned materialists must play the game within these foolish parameters set up prior to our birth that absurdly delineate that there are no perception tools that are independent of the mind. In this case, a flag waving, is the stimulus itself. Outside of the stimulus there is no tangible evidence that the object is or is not there at all. The only basis we have in understanding the world around us are the subjective perceptions that shape and frame the way our minds look at the world in motion. We have exhausted the human mind with the unduly responsibility of believing we are the sole purpose for the universe to exist. Not only have humans failed to cut off the head of the king, humans have failed to cut off the necessity for a law above the universe.

Knowing if the flag exists is impossible beyond the sense perception of the stimulus. We only know by glancing at a flag that there is something that looks like a flag flapping in the wind in front of our eyes. We do not know that the flag exists independent of our eyes. An image of a flag that serves as a stimulus that triggers the brain which then sends information as electricity through our nervous system to the itself. A circular feedback loop constitutes awareness. Can we really know anything beyond this circle of awareness?

Some have called this sort of circular awareness – Suchness. Awareness as visionaries seeing objects in the context of harmony and togetherness with the subject that does the perceiving. Compassionate unity between seer and seen. Universalists and pantheists put forth the belief that there is one substance that unites material existence below the surface. One substance might be called – God which constitutes the foundation of all living beings as varying expressions of this underlying unity. The observable differences among living beings are superficial and a deeper hidden thread of connection ties all of nature and existence together. A fore-runner to unified field theory of consciousness, and it is important to realize that there is a strong desire for the universe and human consciousness as an expression of the universe to find unity with itself.

Becoming-animal, becoming-woman, becoming-mineral, are all phases of resonance in the plateau concept of consciousness. Levels of awareness are plateaus that intensify desire as the subject elevates. These intensities can intensify life and death drives because a world is a war machine and a loving machine. Subjects are world creating device. People in various circumstances bring out different behaviors and affects that are triggered by conditioning. A subject is something altogether different than merely a person. Persons are still clinging to ego consciousness at the level of the 'mind only plateau' of availability to the world.

The stimulus sends information through the nervous system as electricity to the brain. The message is then synthesized and slingshot back to the rest of the nervous system. Is there processing or merely a slingshot? Some understanding of how the mind operates say that it thrives on representations or Mind-Images projected by the object to the brain that then sorts out the information and makes sense of it. What is the basis of this sorting out? What does the brain use to categorize and classify incoming data? Most likely it is based on previous experience. Objects resembling the current object and functioned in a category prior to now will be sorted into the same categories. Perhaps the mind on autopilot is a stereotyping recoding machine. In Deleuze, much like Buddhists, the goal is to ameliorate the representations and Mind-Images that form a barrier, or filter in between the actual (the thing-in-itself) and the virtual (the Mind-Image), to see the object as it is, in its Suchness. This is extremely difficult to do, and it takes years of meditation training to unlearn some of the bad habits that the unenlightened mind has built up. To break free of the fore-structures of consciousness and to illuminate the pure resonance of the object as it shimmers in the Nothingness of the Nothing. Becoming-animal is about the temptation towards violence: "And don't I too carry within me a blood rage, a blindness satisfied by the hunger to mete out blows? How would I enjoy being a pure snarl of hatred, demanding death: the upshot being no prettier than two dogs going at it tooth and nail?" (Bataille, 1998)

As critical animal theorists begin to unravel the different ways that animals interact there is even a new group to discuss inter-species friendships, the basic way that humans interact with one another is through violence. This is because we have historically studied animal behavior through the lens of dominance, submission, violence, as a predator to prey relationship. There are countless other ways that animals relate, and the alienation in the mind-only consciousness, typically involves a totally selfish attitude based on the total eclipsing of all humane, empathetic, social interactions, it is important to open oneself to the object and see it in its fullness. One is too selfish to care about anyone else besides the satiation of ones own base desires, which is historically how animals have been depicted in their natural environment before the enlightenment. The violence of becoming-animal is primal and the only way to have transcendence is to mollify it through detach from detachment which occurs in meditation. To reconnect with the people who are there in one's life. The impulses are always there, but then not giving in to the impulses takes training. Empathy with other people is another way of overcoming the primal impulse towards violence. But, again this means loving someone else more than yourself which is hard to do in a society fixated on the ego. What does this mean? It means that perhaps the dehumanization of our victims has erased any sense of guilt, shame, or grief that many people feel when causing suffering in others. In fact, these negative effects may be so deeply tucked away in the subconscious that the surface level emotions that appear when causing suffering in others seem to showcase a sense of bristling with joy and enthusiasm. A clear sign that the definition of ethics in many people has shifted from compassion to sadism.

Can we still learn to discern certain moral emotions of guilt and shame that should ignite an aggressor with humiliation when seeing the pain on the face of the victim? Selfishness has settled in and become so deeply rooted in the culture of capitalism that the slightest admission of guilt may be impossible for some people. The universality of the ethical discernment in seeing the face of the victim when it suffers is almost unquestionably accepted by Levinas. Ethics is about breaking with habitual spontaneity: "We call this calling into question of my spontaneity by the presence of the Other ethics." (Levinas, 1969, 43). To not give in to the violent impulse by allowing the face of the victim to have an effect. Literally being a stimulus that effects the brain means to have an empathetic response to the Other who is suffering. Ethics is about allowing the other to enter. Which is hard to do because other people may not be as responsible and tactful once they are invited in. Ethics is about hospitality. It means opening a relationship and being a good guest once invited in. A momentary lapse into monism is necessary to overcome the solipsism/narcissism of Mind-Only Consciousness that posits the distinction between subject and object.

The Buddha's palace was full of decadent lies and sensual pleasures that hid the truth about human suffering. Once Buddha went out from the palace and into the world he saw the extreme suffering that existed and developed his philosophy as a way of overcoming the problem of suffering. He had to go out of the consumption and decadence to have his moment of empathy with the sufferers. The problem of suffering is perennial. It is a part of every social order, government, and economy in the history of the world. Suffering was not the historical property of an epoch. It was not particular to this or that time; it was and continues to be a timeless ethical issue.

But like Bob Dylan's *Ballad of a Thin Man*, most people have this sense that things are going terribly wrong, that "there's something happening, but you don't know what it is." The difference between a trained Buddhist Master, and a Marxist vanguard, is that the Buddhist is good with the paradoxes. There is a sense in the tradition of the Koan that the rationalist approach to reality fails to represent the fundamental contradictions in metaphysics. In the promulgating the premature death of metaphysics conflated metaphysics with meta-narratives. This is a purely Western approach to metaphysics as a one-sized fit all set of universal a-priori absolutes that ground ethics and truth. Buddhists in learning to deploy the Koan have unleashed the nihilistic denouement of deconstruction. That reality in its dualism can be both and neither at the same time. Thereby making the tools of logic completely fallible in the face of such metaphysical abstractions. Metaphysics is not about resolving the existential question of "to be, or not to be." It is seeing that we are both beings and non-beings simultaneously. Often it occurs to me that when I admit someone else has a great point and has shared a wonderful idea with me, the other person comes off with the impression that I have just admitted fault in myself. Vice versa, it is brutally difficult for others to admit that "I" have made a wonderful point because it seems to the weak being that there is a flaw in their 'unknowing' of what "I" seem to know. They feel threatened so push harder with their flawed points of view. This "I am right: therefore, you are wrong" mentality is a result of the stupidity of a zero-sum dualistic game. Capitalism thrives on this sort of stupid needless competition that pits ego against ego rather than finding fundamental synthesis with other beings. What this zero-sum dualism does is often make one person feel superior to another, the gracious person winds up in a position of powerlessness due to constantly feeling the need to hand over power to An-Other; and the Other becomes a Self that is in a position of perpetually taking what is offered, therefore this taking Self never really must work on itself; because everything it needs it gets. The selfless and altruistic giving gracious person usually winds up in a constant state of perpetual self-improvement; wondering why their services are ungratefully received. I.e. service as being taken advantage of; this powerlessness is not necessarily only fixable through a shift in consciousness. One must vote with their feet and eventually leave, unless the taker is willing to give back and recharge the batteries of the gracious giver.

In the Buddhist tradition, being and non-being are coterminous. These concepts are enclosed within a common boundary. They are not distinct at all. The gracious giver needs the selfish taker and vice versa. Somehow these personality types have been trained to find each other. As the great Zen Buddhist Van Morrison once said: Chop that wood, carry water, what is the sound, of one hand clapping? Enlightenment, don't know what it is…

# DEVELOP IN SILENT ABIDING

Develop in silent abiding
Discovering emptiness brings fullness
Too much talking, nothing said
Careful talking, discover empty mind
Patience happens, in nothingness
Stop squirming, be still
Settle into skin,
Human doing, becomes human being
Lose prideful attachments
In humility; find the Source of All
Thought blows through untrained mind
Like wind blows through trees
Rustling up leaves and emotions
Trained mind is like tree, bends in wind
Find pivot point, be one with the weather
Powerful storms bring rain, help garden grow
Put no snakes in garden, discipline the mind

Big Sacrifice is Big Love
Give self, until there is no self to give

Within self, infinite reservoir of love
Do not dilute with external objects
Give to heartfelt companions
Make life worth sharing

Praise-Blame temporary
Love-hope springs eternal
Hate kills, Love-hope saves
Big Love overcomes small worries

No status lasts forever
Miniscule mote of dust
In a universe of countless stars

Plant seeds before rain
Gain good roots
Request love with deep sincerity
Give love with equal sincerity
In one speck of dust are vast lands

IT PROBABLY TOOK ME THE FIRST THIRTY YEARS OF MY LIFE TO FI-
nally settle in and feel comfortable in my own skin. Existence is
never tidy. If it seems tidy it is merely a temporary cleanliness of placing
objects in what our minds believe is a perfectly ordered set of forms. Order is temporary and tends towards chaos. Form is void. Void is Form.
In Buddhism if a piece of writing that preserves a particularly important
piece of wisdom it is called a Sutra. In Western religion the term used in
this association would be Scripture. Buddhist Sutras, like sacred scriptures,
are elevated to the status that they are because something in their teachings
reaches beyond the time period in which they were written. These texts
may speak truths that resonate with people in a sort of trans-historical context that may perhaps reach a level of absolution, that makes these truths
applicable in a myriad of times and spaces. One concept that the Buddhist
Sutras mention over and over, again and again are the Skandhas (the senses) – which give us our perceptive connection to the world. A point that
is repeated, again and again in the sutras is that The Five Skandhas (the
senses – sight, sound, smell, taste, touch) are empty. Nothing truer was
ever said, period. The truths that come through from these senses are fleeting – chasing after the next stimuli to excite the senses eventually leaves the
subject feeling like a hollowed-out husk of a human being with nothing of
importance on the inside. Truth comes from the Heart, from within and

happiness is built from the inside of the human being to the outside. Buddha had a few things figured out, because the mind will find a way to fill itself with something, anything, to avoid the emptiness. Meditation on the other hand is retraining the mind to be empty to avoid it being filled with what amounts to intellectual junk food and white noise. Yet, even sitting in silence can become an unnecessary attachment.

Sound becomes a disturbance and disrupts the inner tranquility. One is truly at peace when the subject can turn to a noisy conversation or the exuberance of a child that fills up the room, and remain at peace. When you read you may begin to settle into the unsettling of the silence that surrounds you and that is always already there. For a moment, you may become trapped with your own thoughts. After a while it may become clear that the gifts that the senses bring you are in reality empty forms, but this realization may take time, and for most people, this realization may never happen, because it is with a patient, ponderous, slow moving mind of gravitas (seeing the gravity, the weight, the depth, and the seriousness of the situation) that we begin to see the plain actuality of how dull life actually is, and that is the most terrifying realization of all, which is why most people never get there.

In saying the senses are empty the conclusion I draw is that sensory perception can never bring true satisfaction, only the enhancement of desire. Therefore, there can never be a truly secular Buddhism, because the secular subject still resides in the realm of attachments, and material objects. Senses occasionally give me glimpses of what Immanuel Kant called the 'noumena realm,' the realm beyond the physicality of existence. Most creatures fixate on the phenomenal realm, the realm of what is seen, heard, touched, tasted, and smelled. Yet, there is a cosmic field that records all our thoughts and actions. Once the secular subject detaches from the illusions of the objective so-called 'reality' or the ego-mind, then the subject can tap into forces that are far greater than one mere mortal can imagine.

In working themselves into frenzied chaos the evangelicals who speak in tongues, and act in ways most psychiatrists would call psychotic, may be producing ch'I. Energy pulses coursing through the body as electrical currents sent from the brain through the nervous system, giving off powerful forces. In Aikido, an eastern form of martial arts, masters can flip people without even touching them. This is because they have learned how to harness the power of ch'I it is beside the point to wonder whether it is immanent within the subject or transcendental. It is unimportant whether it derives from God; or the echo chamber of the mind. Ch'I exists and contains force. But, it happens through the attainment of a Samadhi state of deep concentration. As the Heart Sutra begins with the Buddha 'coursing in the deep' the prajna paramita, the Samadhi state, occurs through much practice. Zen masters can will themselves into this state by simply sitting down to meditate. They have so attuned their minds and bodies to be in sync that the mere positioning of the body in a zazen posture, with legs crossed, and back, head, and chest aligned they immediately give off ch'I and go into a deep state of Samadhi.

In capitalist society, the market forces behind its entire ideological apparatus want to always maintain a full mind. It is a function of the behavioral conditioning mechanisms that go into a collective anxiety over the prospect of being empty. Emptiness is the enemy of capitalism, and consumerism. If a subject can live with psychic emptiness, and need not fill the hole in the self with 'stuff' then they are antithetical to the desire towards consumption, or filling up with the next commodity that gives illusory promises of satisfaction. Being good with being empty, in the sense that one can fill the mind with the true vision of deeply held inner-intentions emanating from the cosmic field. As Buddha taught, intentions are the origins of actions. The conformist is constantly misdirected by fads, fashions, and the latest trend in society en masse. Conformists seek intentions externally. Resonate satisfaction from the wellspring within.

Now, in most Christian discourses, the source of this inner-vitality and fullness is of course, God and Jesus. One goes through a series of life calamities, drug and alcohol addiction, sex addiction, partying, various forms of debauchery, that leads one to the conclusion that the sensual pleasures of this world lead only to suffering and heartache. The born again Christian often finds Jesus because they suddenly realize that all of the attempts towards temporary fixes cannot assuage the deep longing in their soul – one must be filled and the 'hole'-complex comes to its ultimate conclusion as the born again Christian fills themselves with God. This myth is so widely disseminated that in my time attending youth groups and Christian summer camps as an adolescent, this theme would crop up in nearly every testimonial given by an evangelical preacher. To think that life conforms to a series of clichés is truly horrifying. Yes, there are some inadequacies in trying to live life from one intense orgasmic experience to the next because it turns experience into a volatile roller coaster. Meditation can help with this by settling the mind, slowing the heart rate, lowering blood pressure, ameliorating the fixation on adrenaline rushes, and dopamine highs.

In my practice meditation, can help the mind pass from moment to moment in appreciation for the experiences that crop up as they pass by, but in a detached, non-judgmental way. Living at peace. It can lead to more profound appreciation for the sense perceptions as the tongue tastes food, as the nose smells a delicate flower, or as the ears listen intently to a beautiful symphony. All the while knowing that the pleasure is temporary, that death sweeps it all away, so the lesson from Mahayana meditation is to be mindful of each moment as it passes. No moment happens twice exactly the same way. Things appear to repeat, but as Karl Marx once said, even history repeats first as tragedy, then as farce. Each repetition carries with it a slight variation on a subtle, yet similar theme. It is being aware of the differences and the similarities that lead the subject to become fully enlightened, or at the very least, mindful of the common spaces occurring in daily life. Moments move through the precariousness of life lived as form and the formlessness in uncanniness of spontaneity.

Negation as negation of static terms and concepts; the movement of new ideas emerges out of the nothingness of time. Precisely because being cannot put a finger on the pulse of time; because time flows through being as the nothing of the nothing the unobjectifiable, non-phenomenal, formlessness that cannot have form, the nothing is the problem of thought. Time is the nothing that forms the problem of thought it thinks with thought and matters to thought without being a matter; it is the matter, without being tangible, without being an object, therefore this precarious ledge that we all stand upon as being moves into the future; is a precarious precipice because time unfolds out into the abyss; and on this ledge, we must move forward reinventing – time is a repetition that is slightly different each time a situation/event occurs. Even the most experienced cosmic-genius lives dangling on the precipice of the future-as-nothing as it becomes real.

Emptiness does not have to be scary. Do you live the same year eighty times, or eighty years once? If each moment is fresh, each year will freshly appear, but to make the moment fresh, one must be aware of the repetitions that cause similar conflicts. Be the pivot point, the center, and the nothing. Be the hole that holds the spokes together and turns the wheel. When you seek, you find, and more importantly, what you seek is often what you find. There is a line written by the great Greek philosopher Heraclitus that seems counter-intuitive, but shows the similarities between Eastern and Western thinking. He says, 'seekers of gold dig up much earth, and find little,' I take the moral to be, those who seek fortune through external objects (gold, money, wealth, prosperity) are looking in the wrong place, and often fail to find true happiness. What you seek is what you will find, is not about seeking material possessions, but internal experiences that lead to true, blissful, long-lasting states of contentment.

Space, or at the very least, the human perception of space is dictated by a matter of proximity to the physical body. In this regard, we usually place limitations on it, and divide it up between the realm of "me" and "not me," but the truth is that space is infinite. There is no distinction between the it and the not it. Up, down, bigger, smaller, east, west, north, south, there is no limit, an astronaut can continue in any direction in outer space at light speed forever and never run out of space. The trick the mind plays is having the subject think that there is a distinction between the outer and inner realm of space. Inside and outside is equally as vast.

Miniscule and enormous spaces are relative. All that we can perceive about the universe might be one cell in a bigger being. One microscopic cell inside of our body could conceivably populate an entire universe inside of us. There is no limit. You contain universes, and universes contain you. The point is to be empty. Be the hole that turns the spokes on the wheel, because the emptiness is connected to the cosmic something that unites us all.

To think that our consciousness is really an amalgamation of our past experiences, and our anxieties about the future, is to forget that we only exist in the present. Memory is a thought image of the past. Emptying the mind of images opens this now and the next now with the gift of its next now as now to simply be, as it is, to present and reinvent silent time as a miraculous gift. A surefire way to remain constantly frustrated is to construct mind-images about what the future should be, rather than accept it as being unpredictable. Things that often give us hope can also not live up to expectations, the things we fear usually do not happen, and the terrible or great events in life are usually things that catch a person completely off guard, because they are impossible to predict. Some people drive themselves mad with regret thinking: "Why didn't I see that terrible event coming?" When no one can positively know, what will tomorrow will bring.

Traditions and taboos are designed to protect us from the unexpected by giving people guideposts by which they can inform their daily decisions. But these social constructs cannot make someone good. This is because goodness cannot be imposed upon someone externally. To be good means to extinguish impulsive and self-destructive behaviors, which takes resiliency, and discipline. To break old destructive habits, one must construct new habits. Traditions are cultural habits. Good traditions are relative to each culture, but ethics and virtue are both cultivated from within, through practice.

The question becomes, can goodness blossom in the shadow of evil? Being in good company helps someone be good, but what about when the environment is evil? True virtue is a light that shines from within and even in dark places the desire to do good bursts through. Virtue is independence, or rather, non-dependence upon circumstantial situations. To be truly good, one does not depend upon outward expressions of praise. Goodness is something one simply does based on an inward compulsion, an inner drive. If you are good in the expectation of receiving a reward, you miss the point of being good, because goodness is its own reward.

Energy used in conflict dissipates, and turns to garbage in the mind. It manifests as anxiety, and is dispelled into nothing. Energy used in love is never wasted; it multiplies, grows, expands and changes the organism and its environment. Love is the overarching feeling of the Tao, in the sense that no effect rises when everything is as ease. Sitting quietly, easing the mind, allows the love that hides underneath everything to ease the body and trickle up through to the surface. Everything that endures does so because someone loved it and made a commitment to keep it alive, not as an attachment, but as a relation of love. Not out of panic if the thing were to pass on, but as a persistent commitment to nourish and develop in connection with all living things.

The brain becomes the kind of order that the self creates for it. If neurotic, loud, bombastic order is all that the self puts in front of the mind, then the mind will resemble those traits. Neurosis in the brain is a result of chaos in the social order. In neurosis, there is order and the brain accepts that order if that is all that is put in front of the brain. If fear is all that put in front of the brain, then fear is what it will become. If love and affection is what you put in front of the brain then that is what the brain will be, it manifests what it contemplates, and it contemplates what exists before it. Nourish the brain by being fully present in your environment, which means removing the toxic energy before it reconstitutes the fabric of your mind.

The best way to do this is to practice listening. Quietly listening can do better than being at one with the neurotic noise in our daily lives. Listen, but do not hear, because the sound, like all things in this world, does not exist. Conflict arises when the mind thinks it is separate from the other being that it hurts. Hurting others hurts the self. Killing kills the soul of the killer as much as the victim.

Do you use your relationships to avoid being alone? Fear of being alone with yourself means you will become a stranger even to yourself. Remember, the one person who is with you always is yourself. No one else can dream your dreams, feel your feelings, and think your thoughts. So, befriend yourself. Feeling comfortable in your own skill will be the greatest gift you can receive. Finding people who you can share that gift with is to find true companionship.

And, always remember that the time you have in this life is finite. Never act like you have all the time in the world to accomplish your goals. The paradox about time is that the time in life is finite, but eternity is always already available to anyone at any moment. Eternity is not merely available after death, eternity is now here and nowhere. This may seem like a tricky point, but in my experience, the person who compares what is said with what he already knows, cannot learn. Learning is the realization that "I", or what appears as the "I", does not know; therefore, it is a process of seeking to know. Love is not knowledge, but non-attachment, at least in the sense of loving wisdom, rather than data, trivia, and information. Attachment leads to co-dependence and dysfunctional experiences like jealousy, pride, envy, greed, all of which are empty wasted emotions.

Love requires some level of personal and social autonomy. Love is the freedom to simply be. No one ever says that they 'become' in love, but rather that they are in love, love is being, not becoming. If you believe in love as becoming, then becoming is an attachment to an illusion of what a person might be, rather than seeing what the person is. Always focus on what is, not what might be, or should be, or could be. Those things are illusions of an ego that idealizes, rationalizes, and deludes itself into the narcosis of escapism. The reality is too painful to see so the ego pretends as if it does not exist, or that it will someday change, and improve. People can improve nevertheless there is no guarantee that anyone ever will. Enlightenment happens precariously and no one can be forced to see the light. Enlightenment must be voluntary, accepted through your own volition.

To find the light one must accept that the clear majority of human beings on this planet are living in a state where their inner and outer chaos are connected. If all you set before your mind is outward chaos, if that is all that you focus on, then that is what the mind will become. Inner chaos leads to fear, and to vanquish the fear people turn to all sorts of mystical experiences. Yet, the irony is that what is needed is not what is sought, you cannot pursue a quiet peaceful mind. Listening and sitting quietly, literally turning off the mind is what is needed, rather than a mystical band-aid over the pain and escapism through pursuit of the next mindless spectacle or amusement.

The great German philosopher Theodor Adorno once wrote that modern capitalism is nothing more than an "open air prison." I believe what he meant by this is that no individual can exist without money or earning a wage, which basically makes everyone in capitalism a prisoner of the marketplace. To survive the realities of capitalism, one must give up most of his daily existence toiling in labor, usually to enrich someone else. Greed has a way of trickling in to all aspects of life in capitalism. Everyone must provide a good or service to maintain their daily bread, but new needs emerge all the time. Commodities that did not exist a few years ago, become so predominant that life without them seems virtually unimaginable. For this simple reason, most people look at me like a crazy person when I say that I do not own a cell-phone. This is an attachment that leads to a noisy cluttered mind and I refuse to buy into that mindset.

The neurotic mind is a thief pretending to be a policeman that catches itself – a vicious cycle. Stop the cycle break free by disavowing needless attachments. Stop the dualism that separates mind from body, subject from object, us from them. Consciousness is the result of the content that it unifies with, and it unifies with what is in the environment. Remake the environment by secluding yourself every now and then, delving into meditation can be offer this graceful seclusion. There is no one else who can feel your pain, or experience your joy. Let no one rob you of the temple that is there once you step within the inner bliss and harmony of the quiet mind. Pleasure exists temporarily. It is here and then gone. Love springs eternal.

# Docile Bodies

FALSE CONSCIOUSNESS IS ACTUAL TRUE BELIEF THAT YOU ARE FREE Freedom is ignorance towards the forces that determine the course of our lives

Saying the course of our lives are determined by forces outside of our control

is not the same as saying there is planning and intelligence behind these forces?

or that these forces are metaphysical, these forces appear to be the most natural way,

which is orderly, reflexive, and so clearly outside of our control, which conceals a deeper level of worrisome chaos permeating all who are aware of the flow of these unplanned forces of nature...

Major life investments we "must" make to become free – home, car, college education.

Major sources of debt that keep us chained to a job in fear – home, car, college education.

Technology is sold to consumers as 'caring for yourself' – you need that cellphone to compete for that job, you owe it to yourself to get that tablet it brings you joy, so many self enhancement projects are available to you once you get online, we care so much about you the consumer we invent these gadgets because we care about making your life better, technology is sold do you, for the sake of 'progress' (forget about profits!) forget how tired you are, how comfortable you've become, how your brain is turning to jell-o, how you've forgotten how to think, how you've become a 'docile body' because everything comes to you so easily...forget history, forget human contact, forget...to learn..."We" the all knowing, all seeing, omniscient, omnipresent overseers of the 'good' moral New World Order want what is best for our flock, think of the jobs we create, the taxes we produce, the products which satiate a need, forget about the dwindling rainforest and the plumes of smoke billowing from consistent churning factories (there are no jobs remember? There is no production, remember? We are post-industrial, this is a wasteland, remember?) forget the jobs relying on the destruction of the environment...see, taste, touch, smell, hear, feel, and fill your senses with the joy of consumption...enjoy! It is your "God" given right! Forget that there are too many people, think of all the jobs we are creating, the economies we are producing, the lives we are conducting, and remember there is a reason why things happen...

As I TOOK A MORNING to stroll through a small park that nobody knew about near my suburban neighborhood the daisies blooming, the robins gathering worms, grass sprouting among the sugary flowing maples, I wandered through a broad meadow thinking to myself in a voice that sounded like a grizzled Charles Bukowski: "Why are all these creatures busying themselves? For what? Where are they going and in such a thoughtless hurry?" Happening upon a burrow next to a gate stretched over a trickling and glistening little creek bed I saw an old man. When we passed, we exchanged glances. Trenchcoated, leaning out as if from an alley, half concealed he muttered a sound that resounded from a distant memory perhaps from a childhood echo chamber, forgotten by time. "Child, my child. Beware the body, you will miss it when it goes, it is to be used for chasing monarchs in the spring, basking in the sun of summer, swimming, competing, glistening with the glow of love, gathering walnuts in the fall, hauling in the harvest with oxen plow, only in the final days do we nestle in if we are lucky with soothing libations near a wood burning fireplace as this gives temporary respite from the cold harsh inevitable winter, hopefully in solace with someone we love, or who can still love despite the crushing burdensome inertia of total apathy saturating the world." Speechless I stared into his glowing eyes with a glassy eyed wonder that reflected the light as he continued: "Son! Most fools think that fear of death keeps us alive. No, they could not be further from the truth the whole truth and nothing but the truth. Hunger my boy, fear of hunger is the most noble motivation of a scoundrel. Nothing could be the most noble harbinger of evil besides the drive to eradicate hunger, in the self, in others, in the entire dim world. To be full, fat, happy, apathetic, and to discover contentment prior to the last fulfilling joy. Live not as the death suckers, feeding off the takers taking being as grasshoppers who spring joyfully through the meadow in the sunshine of ignorance, unable to count the withering blades of grass in the ever-narrowing field. What gifted person, lives by shining, joy is their lighthouse, dashes to safe harbor in the forever sleep of night?"

When he ceased talking aloud I walked across the gated bridge as a fellow trespasser crossed over the river this ghost disappeared into nothing behind the slippery elms as if our mutual existence constituted a brief interlude between realistic mystic shadows. Specters anticipating each other on the path to the cross over and beyond the now. I said to myself: "Eye for an eye makes the whole world blind. Yet, you still wind up dead when you turn the other cheek. The Way is not entirely a peaceful way. There is not one moment in our waking lives that we are not giving away now for the sake of a pleasure that is yet to come; and a-way and rather the Way of the now is in the subsistence and persistence of rendering access to pleasure. As soon as we find awareness of this moment this moment is gone onto the next moment. Who cares what is it for? To forage your whole life to perhaps find a few fleeting scraps of joy and mountains upon mountains of suffering in between." I cut him off: "We cannot know nor claim to know what the future will be. Since we do not know what the future will value until it happens it seems safe to say that it concerns me without being my concern." Might as well just sit and eat Lotus like those fools suffering their 'illness' of substance induced narcolepsy from the Odyssey. Trying in their own desperate ways to avoid the miserable fact that our lives are unavoidably our own. We cannot swap places – and the body is the prison of the soul. Or is it the other way around – the soul is the prison of the body? Is our physical form what traps and limits the spirit of our soul? Or, is the imprinting of moral values onto the soul something that limits the experimental behavior one may take to test the limits and intensify the pleasures of the soul? I guess it depends on how you were raised and whether or not you have a spirit of adventure in you, whether you view morals as a crutch for the fearful and the weak, or whether you have a sturdy foundation of right and wrong.

For many years growing up in a Judeo-Christian society, reading the philosophies that were either an outgrowth or a response to that belief system. It was obvious that the body was understood as an object to be punished, tortured, and at best modestly repressed. Western Societies, although often more open than some other places in the world, are usually 'despisers of the body' – we hate our bodies. Correcting the imperfections in our bodies often involves torturous exercise, dieting, malnourishment, or worse plastic surgery.

Bodies are laden with possibilities. It is no use to sit and wonder what a body can do if we do not know by now. Often when I read the Ancient

Buddhist Sutras the wisdom that filters through to my modern mind often valorizes a sense of stillness. Somehow, in an era where sedentary culture is a way of life, the lack of stillness and sitting is not the major problem. People get more than enough sitting still in a typical day. America has become a passive society of observers. It is the way we sit that bothers me. Usually hovering over a computer, at a desk in a cubicle, or watching propaganda on television, or any number of other ways of sitting sedentary while white noise carries on around us. Apathy amid amusement at all time seems to be the confusion we life amidst in a society that constantly says, "Yes!" Control can be placed on people through restricting or loosening access to the things that bring us pleasure in life. Unfortunately, if you can obtain easy access to all of life's necessities by sitting in one place, people will choose to sit in one place. The arc of history bends towards happiness and if access to happiness is easier and easier, this means the arc of history bends towards being-inactive. The abundance of sitting is one thing, the lack of reflective silence is another, and finally the dead ends and black holes where actual reflection takes us. Getting up and moving can remedy some of the reflective malaise. Perhaps walking during a yoga hike in nature could help. Do we also cater our exercise towards a militaristic physique? Musculature among men as a remnant of a warrior society that predates modern militarism, going back to the warring Sparta society that brought up its men to be tough Stoic warriors with what they believed to be impenetrably thick-skinned attitudes towards each other.

The militarism of contemporary society has subjected the system of inscription, where anyone can become a soldier, to extreme rationalization. Rationalization means to make things most efficient. It means to set up rules and prevent any unexpected events through increased control. In fact, modern military power relies on the belief that anybody can become a soldier. Useful bodies are necessary to capitalism to have a source of labor capable of performing the work necessary to maintain a stable economic base. Docile bodies are necessary so there is no opportunity to rise in revolt. Docile bodies are molded into passive people who will do the work necessary to maintain the production processes in the currents of the economy. This is a very tricky problem for ethicists who also do political theory because these docile useful bodies tend to be completely complacent with regards to anything beyond a monetary exchange for their labor. Buddhist meditation tends to have a rather bad reputation for feeding on this consumer mentality by creating lackadaisical apathetic couch potatoes who want solutions to just occur to them out of thin air. Sweat equity loses its meaning.

Enhancing therapeutic techniques that regulate pathology, objectifying pathos as something biological, chemical, and classifying it as an illness. Subordinating instinctive drives into a sublimation of creative and productive pursuits. This is the promise and curse of civilization. Discontents are always latent in the murky depths of the unreflective unconscious mind. Civilization carries with it the burden of deferring base instinctual pleasure in the here and now for a greater reward in the future.

What media and politics offers to the common worker is often nothing more than a way to channel the discontents of unfulfilled phantasies of those currently stuck in a life of mostly needless toil. It is foolish to dismiss unconscious drives as a symptom of neurotic housewives with ample time to sit around and complain about this or that little discomfort. The 'princess and the pea' interpretation of talk therapy is how I view political discourse offered by the media. Often one gets glimmers of small reformist-prescriptive measures to put a finger in the dam to temporarily offset the oncoming inevitability of a total collapse of the capitalist system of exploitation, suffering, and enormous stripping of wealth from the clear majority of human beings on this planet. One watches the media and political pundits dance on a thousand pins as they fail to engage with the fundamental solutions. Time and time again we are given pseudo-solutions that never consider how transforming the economic structure of a society would lead to a change in human social relations. Everyone talks past everyone else. If you spend your life in such a hurry to obtain happiness, you might just rush right past it. Enlightenment has absolutely nothing to do with occupational therapy.

Language can even become a sort of prison system. Incredibly, this is imbedded into the structure of language itself – as the French terms for grammar and syntax are 'langue' and 'parole' to get out on parole one must utilize language correctly, but one never fully escapes from the watchful eye of the praetorian guard hovering over correcting improper usages of this or that term. Embedded deep into the subconscious memories from our childhood, if we had a so-called proper education. One a more nefarious level the censorship of ideas does not have to occur through the overt announcement that some ideas are being censored and others are not, simply closing off the circulation of this or that idea, or closing off the pipeline of ideas that may form a basis on this or that word, or a set of principles, or concepts, by simply closing off the flow of ideas and allowing some words to fall out of popular circulation means that those who control the channels of communication have an incredible amount of power. Power over and within knowledge and how power/knowledge is produced. You do not have to burn the books you just remove them.

Life is not determined by consciousness, but consciousness by life. If consciousness becomes what it becomes after life emerges then the hypothesis here is that consciousness is stamped out by life circumstances. Race, gender, and class play a more impactful role in the development of character than say personal ambition and determination as the drive and motivation to succeed. There are economically determining factors that may be the most prominent features in the development of consciousness. Consciousness may be circumscribed by conditions not of its choosing and therefore formed from a basis that it did not freely construct on its own.

In this situation, of course a brutal 'law of the jungle' mentality where life outside of the social contract created and enjoyed by wealthy bourgeois business interests creates conditions where life is 'nasty, brutish, and short.' In other words, violent and competitive consciousness is a by-product of horrifically exploiting conditions of existence produced by the destitution created at the margins of capitalism. The limit of capitalism is slavery. Consciousness develops after the facts of life occur, which is usually happenstance outside of the control of merely one individual. Having the good fortune to be born into a wealthy family during a time of peace will certainly afford more opportunities than being born into a peasant family in a war-torn area where the net income is $100 a year. Life prospects are much grimmer if someone is born into the second scenario. Opportunities for nourishment of mind and body are less likely because human beings in the second scenario are scrapping day after day to find their next meal just to survive.

This view may also assume that human consciousness is subject to the inertia of the ebb and flow of life, that consciousness is throw-ness into life. Human beings are blank slates inscribed upon by the material conditions into which they find themselves born. This is a rather limp 'docile' view of the human body itself in that humans are described as lacking the personal ingenuity to create life in their own terms. Human consciousness evolves as society develops. Marcuse fuses this materialist view with Sigmund Freud held a view that there were innate instinctual drives in the human organism which were subject to historical modification. Instinctual drives such as the sex drive, the drive to satiate hunger, the drive to keep a roof over your head, the desire to feel love and a sense of belonging were all subject to historical modification. All of these instinctual drives, of which there are too many to list here, seek to find some sort of mental or intellectual as well as somatic, bodily, corporeal, or physical manifestation.

Writing as a direct outgrowth of these new emerging critical theories in the early 1960's Michel Foucault began from the perspective that human nature is now completely surrounded, determined, enmeshed, imprisoned, and/or incarcerated by the social milieu an individual inhabits. A milieu is an artificial environment created in modern times that has completely taken human beings away from their primal natural instincts. A step beyond arguing that man has repressed instincts that fail to find gratification, Michel Foucault argued that perhaps even the way modern man imagines these primal instincts is a social product. Often one of the only statements that people know about him is taken out of context when he says that he argues in favor of the death of man; but it is precisely my previous statement about his position that allows him to say that with full confidence. Even the understanding of what constitutes a human being is created under artificial circumstances. There is no historical origin that mankind can get back to and become free, there is no Garden of Eden and so forth. The milieu does not necessarily repress instincts as much as completely stripping instincts of their natural qualities.

There is another side to this discussion that seems to be lost on many people and that is the hidden secret in all of this is that capitalism can control people precisely by giving consumers what they want, or think they want. A much more powerful mechanism for totalitarian control is anti-repression. Rather than control by setting up sacred taboos and shouting "No!" or "Thou Shalt Not!" Social control is much harder to resist when it shouts "Yes!" "Do As You Wish!" When power shifts from repressing instinctual drives to releasing these drives, there is a new terrain where power effects the productive, expressive relational aspects of daily lives.

As was once said, the obstacle is the way. When all obstacles inhibiting the gratification of instinctual desires are removed, all bets are off! Power then animates the docile bodies. The major impediment to liberation is not overcoming apathy but knowledge that seriousness can overcome all evils. Compassion and gratitude can overcome all feelings of hopelessness in the midst of a culture that tells us we can have it all even though spatially, temporally, the mere finitude of time allotted in life makes this virtually impossible. There are only so many places one can go in life and only so much time one has to spend in pursuit of life goals. Make haste and more importantly make priorities.

A seemingly endless supply of consumer products serves to mollify the exploited classes instinctual drives as well as focus attention on the pleasures of consumption and recharge ch'I depleted during the toils of production. As the Christian saying goes 'the mind is willing, but the flesh is weak' seems a bit of an oversimplification of what is going on there and I prefer what the great Italian communist revolutionary Antonio Gramsci claimed was necessary to push against the current wave of capitalist stupidity in saying what was needed then and is needed now is pessimism of the intellect, optimism of the will.

# Producing Being

WITHIN MOST FORMS OF SOCIAL CONTROL THERE IS A PRODUC-tive quality to power relations. There is always a framework to power relations that conceals the dimensions of the structures that make up the groundwork of the framework. Often the moral transgression of some unwritten and invisible rule causes power to become visible, transgression can draw power out into being a presence; into a being that is aware of power. Frameworks of power constitute the invisible prisons outside of which one may feel tinges of remorse, guilt, shame, and negative effects that may indicate the point which the subject faithlessly traverses beyond the gaze of God. An allegedly all-seeing eye that cannot be seen but corrects behavior through the invisible hand of its immanent conscience. Eyes can see out but cannot see into the mind. In no uncertain terms, the structure of the invisible framework of the metaphysics of Christian jurisprudence IS the material prison. We now see this metaphysics decomposing before our very eyes. Truth is you and I are all God. The God phrase: "I am that I am" is the most powerful mantra of self-manifesting ever discovered. Learning means learning to remain undisturbed and undistracted from the "I am that I am" that you want to manifest, amusements are only one small aspect of the distractions that emerge when one distills the depth of this manifesting quality. In a society where the pictures are provided it must be presumed that a very common chakra deficiency entails the deadening of the third eye, the chakra that guides our creative spirit through visualization. What we visualize manifests.

Almost every totalitarian dictator in history has given people bread, circuses, and open sources of pleasure as a way of life. While repression can be a powerful tool to control people by saying, "No!" to desires, an even more nefarious tactic of social control is exerted through saying, "Yes!" Control through loosening morals and opening the channels of desire that have long been repressed. In capitalism power is maintained by the subordinate relation of the worker within the process of production and the maintenance of capitalist hegemony over the modes of production. Within assembly line industrial production, the worker is subjugated into a position of being a prosthetic extension of the virtuosity of the machine that performs the process of production. Assembly line work rationalizes the processes of production that take up most of the time in our daily lives. Some countries, including Germany, are now mandating that companies must have a fair balance of workers and women on the board of directors. What this does is give a fair and balanced perspective on how the operations should be run. If the CEO's and accountants handle the balance sheets without understanding the concerns of workers, then there are limitations to what knowledge has an impact on power. Limitations under which we can be producing beings and which beings are allowed at the helm of production.

In artisanal modes of production, the worker is master over the tool by skillfully utilizing knowledge of all aspects of production from beginning to end. Industrial capitalism changes the role of the typical worker to the point where labor is characterized by repetitive tasks performed by the worker with little skill required. The virtuosity, that is mastery over all aspects of production from beginning to end, is no longer a property of the worker, as it was in artisanal production. Instead, virtuosity is in the machine and the mechanization of the production process subsumes the worker to the point where the worker is entirely void of any skill set that would provide sustenance outside of the market. The worker is a cog in the machine of the production process, completely dependent on the machine to produce commodities for consumption. The workers must go to market to sustain their basic needs. Workers are in a precarious position of propertylessness. The worker is excluded from ownership of the modes of production and lives without owning land. In addition, the worker has no method of sustenance outside of the subjectivity of the market and has no identity outside of the market. Sustaining oneself outside of capitalism is not only unfeasible, it is unthinkable and the workers' dependency on the market totalizes the workers' autonomy. Production and producing beings mirror the reality of the needs of the beings that are being produced, because the beings that are being produced are being produced-for, that is, the beings that are produced-for possess the needs that are considered in the production process.

On the other hand, there is a precarious position for capital as the economy becomes deregulated and informal. As workers are displaced without being reabsorbed into the economy they are forced to become versatile to survive. This is a completely undesirable process yet Marx and more recent theorists have postulated that this is a necessary process that will transform the worker at a micro-political level.

It has been passed down since the classical understanding that essence was somehow created prior to existence. The nature of man is inherently self-interested but through reflection humans can overcome the "state of nature" to create a functional civilization where people are given the freedom to flourish as the rational, self-interested, citizens that they were created to become. Even though there is nature, this does not mean there is an intelligence hidden behind nature.

Logic became a way to apply reason to the topsy-turvy seemingly chaotic cogitations of nature, and many philosophers began to move away from discussions of nature in favor of logic as technique to develop and harness the power of nature. A growing thought process turned into a full-blown movement that occurred in the same historical moment as the invention of psychiatry, psychology, and later came sociology. The transition of substituting the study of nature for logic was a major move. Many civilizations have gone through this change. In the West it happened several times, most recently during the French and German Enlightenment Periods in the late 18$^{th}$ century. In China, it happened towards the end of the 'Warring States Period' and in both instances it marked a transition from relative homeostasis to radical changes. In both cases philosophers believed that the shift from studying nature as if it were an unchanging object to studying logic as the fundamental instrument by which to understand the world around us gave philosophers, scientists, political leaders, and even laypeople immense power. What occurred was that philosophy substituted one 'truth' regime for another and this interpretation may imply that logic is nothing more than the temporary repression of nature. When people believe that Logic is an indication of progress this is based on a privileged position of selfhood from within a historical time-period when logic has arisen as a dominant indication of power/knowledge. Those who can use logic can harness nature, which becomes a valuable skill among leaders of industry. Even though there was this newly sought emphasis on logic as a tool for progress, there were many who simply could not think logically, or be trained in the applications of logic.

This transition where intellectuals moved from discussing human nature, to utilizing logic as a method of perhaps improving nature (be it, human nature, or technological apparatuses to extract value from nature as a source of resources); impacted all areas of life.

The interpretation of mental illness as transforming the individual into a mechanical appendage was most apropos as Western economies transitioned from agrarian to industrial modes of production with mechanized forms of mass production. The insinuation became clear. Mental illness shuts down individual subjectivity. The illness completely disintegrates the individual's ability to think rationally and act for oneself. The illness transforms them into beings maintained by bodily life alone. This is a misappropriation of illness creating a totalizing narrative regarding illness that is a bit simplistic. Mental illnesses tend to move from periods of latency to manifestation where the nervous condition is manageable or completely controlling the individual it afflicts to a period where the individual is at the mercy of the condition. In most cases health and illness work in stages and levels of intensity. On certain days' people feel better or worse depending on different conditions.

Can sanity survive while living in insane conditions? One of the primary goals of Romantic poetry was to facilitate inner experience, and an individual relationship with itself and its object of study, in this situation it would be the self. The discovery of the reflective self perhaps coincided with the disappearance of mass carnival experiences. Immanence was overtaken by transcendence and sublimation as the dominant and preferable cultural experience.

What was interesting was that at this same time, there was a transition in production from locating virtuosity in the individual artisan to the mechanized mode of production in the factory. The virtuosity of the production process is in the machine rather than the worker. Madness results when the worker begins to mimic the behavior of the machine by completely internalizing their subjectivity rather than sublimating it into an immanent cultural experience provided by a carnivalesque experience. A playful experience with a few funhouse mirrors thrown in for a good measure of confusion. In early industrial production, there was still a mysticism that was alive and well on the eve of such poems as the Sorcerer's Apprentice that was a poem about a sorcerer's apprentice who casts a spell that makes his mop self-aware enough to mop the floor on its own without even laying a human hand on it; and William Blake's famous line about the new rise of mass production offered by the 'dark satanic mills' of capitalism that locked workers in for most of the day. Today, there are even remnants of this nostalgic utopian mysticism that life could arise without turmoil by being unburdened with the pressures of work that grind down mind, body, and soul. Some new utopians are called 'Fully-Automatic Luxury Communists' or "Accelerationists" who push for fully automated labor to free up labor from the 'oppression of time' as I call it, but rather than harnessing the power of magical sorcery, man now truly believes all this can be accomplished through harnessing the power of science, medicine, and so forth. Yet, how can one argue against the plain simple argument that the high-minded seriousness of this proposition that calls itself 'modern' leads to stern marching around, busying oneself all day, trying to solve all sorts of insoluble problems, an intensification of affect that some say was integral not foreign to the rise of Fascism in the twentieth century (i.e. the Frankfurt School).

As the industrial mode of production becomes increasingly repressive and production becomes excessively mechanical displacing the necessity of labor power in the production process the likelihood for revolution by the property-less workers is substantially increased. This revolutionary subjectivity is intensified even more when workers aren't reabsorbed into the productive process. Marx predicted that this property-less situation of the worker paves the way for a transformation of society altogether. As modernity becomes increasingly repressive, that is as capitalism or other state controlled economies become pervasive this may create circumstances that are a pressure cooker for psychosis and other nervous conditions. Impatient beings act the part of impatience. Spending money even though they do not have any money.

Rushing around living ad hoc from moment to moment rather than patiently, diligently, planning life moves and then taking opportunities as they arise. Frenetic inspiration turns to passion of undisciplined impulsivity. As they say in some Eastern philosophy; enlightened ones see the same cow a thousand times with fresh eyes. Every time you see the same cow it is a new cow.

*Let not the beauty of the everyday become less than beautiful merely because you are blessed enough to see it every day.*


GREETING LIFE WITH enchantment means you create enchanting possibilities. Producing being is produced out of a self-caused-room: the mind. Seeds planted in previous lives (even the previous lives within this incarnation); cause the groundwork for the dharma practices in this life. Karmic redemption from past behaviors turn to habits in the present moment. In such a situation, one might argue as Bernard Stiegler does quite convincingly, that the memory work necessary for learning and mastery is more and more becoming outsourced to digital databases. Reliance on the brain as the engine of virtuosity has been superseded by the reliance on digital power and database storage, which has become the new 'archive'; the new memory, the new cultural history, and provided the new cultural amnesia even though there is less and less possibility of active forgetting in the digital era when every nook and cranny of history has been exposed. Whether people are getting dumber because life is allegedly getting easier is one thing, whether the problems of disease, war, greed, and violence are completely and universally solvable is another.

The relevant questions become clear. What will revolution look like and at what level does the transition from capital take place? Perhaps it will not take the form of previous revolutions in the sense of a historical moment such as the event of the French Revolution. Perhaps it will instead be the result of an abundance of free play to the point where people can imagine externalities to capitalism.

What can be perceived or what can be sensed is called into question with the labor of creating a new sense of oneself as an aesthetic being, a being producing one's own sense of beauty. Freedom is nothing if it is not the freedom to live at the edge of limits where all comprehension breaks down. This is the micro-political level where individuals take the space to creatively express a revolution at the level of their being. This sort of revolution does not take the form of an armed insurrection, but many little revolutions at the level of creative expression that disintegrate the conventions of language to the point where language itself is stammered. Stammering of language puts expression outside of the prison-house of the self-caused-room. Signification that no longer revolves around a centralized and standardized meaning. The falcon that no longer hears the falconer and flies free and wild. A circle in time as circumlocution to give expenditure that preserves the immutable difference/deference of language. A circle in time as the languages we use as currency circulating through the body-electric, the body-politic. Loose-ends bonding-tying-keeping an economy of language to escape into open to multiple interpretations.

Cutting ties between classes. A new elevation of political consciousness on a collective level will entail a scission or rupture with the capitalist mode of production while retaining its heritage of highly developed technology and science. In this interpretation of revolution there is an ontological and economic shift that occurs, a rupture with capitalism, while retaining aspects of the economy that accelerate production and develop the general intellect. In this way, the transition to communism is a historical change, that is a change of the elements of the social order which are purely derived from human will and volition while maintaining much of the same façade of familiar technologies and science. We are all part of the same sea – and yet, we are unique singular drops.

The recognition that one seeks and needs in this life is not entirely understood as praise or honor bestowed upon oneself by a more powerful being. Although these may be powerful motivational factors in life these are not the only ways to make sense of our desire for recognition. Re/cognition is an association between beings where the horizon line of apperception is delimited, or opened to create a space for intersubjective social relations. For some the boundary of the self exists at the level of immediate consciousness and direct experience. What is merely present, the presence of being. Being as presence shifted in the twentieth century with the emergence of new technologies that allowed worldwide communication; now, the 'center is elsewhere' in the ontological construction of the being of beings. We can watch news from around the world, have access to virtually any type of art, music, film, or book. It is a magnificent time and a horrifying time. Magnificent because of the knowledge at our fingertips. Horrifying because on one level we are less and less able to compute all this data, we outsource memory work to computers, and we are slowly alienating ourselves from our immediate experience as perpetual transportation elsewhere kills epistemological desire to transcend the known; and look to televisual experts to tell us what we/they need us to know.

Language is always already discourse and conversational. Whenever someone opens into conversation one leads oneself open to dis/course; that is to disrupt the course of one's mind-only-stream-of-consciousness. The Other who you open yourself up to re/flects, that is, returns the topic to you as a redirection a re/volutionizing or routinizing a change in the flow of the circularity of self-oriented conversations. Ideas represent consciousness. Giving ideas to the world means one loses consciousness.

Consciousness leaves only to bounce off the other (the other is a rubbery, bouncy other) and springs the idea back in a new form. Changed by the process of passing through another mind before it returns. This is recognition i.e. RE-cognition or changing the cognitive process by which we understand the world; this is intersubjective knowledge; this is what some have called dialectics. Dialectics being consciousness re-cognized back to itself, connective consciousness reuniting with itself through language, ideas, art, music, philosophy, so forth. Since the ground of the connection is language and the ground of consciousness is ego the dialectical nature of the discursivity of the connection is tenuous at best. Language brings us together and we ourselves may tear us apart. This process of unification and division occurs over and over, again and again – this dialectical process is what we call progress.

Capitalism is mere money becoming one with itself again and again. No new ideas are put into circulation. Co/modification is man changing nature into a usable form, usable for man. Man, changes nature, and what man creates also changes man. For instance, with farming came increased availability of food, more caloric intake occurred, some of this went to brain development, some went to body development. Voila humans developed highly functional frontal lobes and grew taller and perhaps more obese in size from time to time. Consciousness is deepened by improved material conditions but only if those resources are channeled to activities that operate and function to deepen consciousness. Re/cognition and communication is one of those processes rather than mere resuscitation of rote memorized trivia. Zen-being-the-nothingness of the countless gold to a merry heart. Happy sparrow alone and free. Flying high in the darkening cloudy sky.

Some other critics of this type of social revolution is that it posits a purely "Modern" understanding of progress and revolution. It is a superficial sort of revolution that does not go far enough to transform society at its core. This sort of gradualism and reformism of the modes of production is informed by a binary opposition of ideas that privileges the modern at the expense of the pre-modern. Perhaps there is no looking back. When we look back it is not back on an authentic view of the past. Past-life regressions are distorted through the gaze of the present. Learning distorts the past. Fresh eyes of experience give new and unnatural perspectives on the past. To posit a revolution that turns back the hands of time is to fall into the trap of impossible return based on the longing of nostalgia. Remember, nostalgia yearns for a return and is motivated by a current based in anguish. Something has gone horribly wrong for the person who yearns to go back in time.

Far from arguing that revolution will result in a return to pre-modern economics such as feudalism the critics who ran counter to this line of reasoning would say that the privileging of Modern sensibilities (advanced technology and science) is to retain the rationalist logic that inheres to the logic of the State. This implies that capitalism is a necessary step along the way for the transition to something beyond itself. This is because capitalism provides the developed technology and science necessary to make modernity function. The factories and technologies that allow for communication are necessary for any movement of progress into the future. Most economists and Marxists agree that there is something different about the modern era than all previous eras. This amounts to the mass production of goods in factories which utilize the division of labor and machinery to produce more goods at a lower price. Which is coupled with the regulatory mechanisms that maintain an orderly production process. The newest thing is the expansion of this ethos of regulation into all aspects of society.

This is including even personal ethics, religion, science, to the point where the modern subject is under constant surveillance and internalizes the regulatory ethos as if it were its own moral conscience.

In a society in which production is still regulated by advanced technology there would have to be a class of experts trained to maintain this accelerated sort of production. Undoubtedly there would be a hierarchy at the level of knowledge production in which the people who have superior knowledge would have superior wages, power, prestige, because they would be essential to the productive functions of this future society.

If a revolutionary were to take a novel perspective on revolution. A society so free that it circulates the disintegration of sense among all people. Perhaps then revolution would be so thorough that the future would no longer resemble the present of capitalist mode of production. In fact, the future might be such a radical mutation that our conceptions of economy would be altered to the point where societies and civilizations may take a complete departure from economy as the basis for its ideological superstructure.

What is needed to perform this revolution is a new rationality as a complete rupture with everything we currently perceive as rational. The previous historical revolutions of America, France, and Russia have started this trend by establishing societies that were based on constituent power, at least in principle at their conception. Constituent power is boundless. Its only measure is the limitlessness of the multitude, the absolute versatility of its relations, and the powerful and constitutive interrelations that compose its real dynamic. From beginning to end the entire process of sovereignty has been transcendental to the point where there is little more than historical inertia (with all the ideological trappings of the superstructure) keeping the system afloat. The modes of production that constitute capital are precarious and heterogeneous. If Nicholas Poulantzas was correct, capitalism will not survive as a totalitarian state. It thrives on soft power is its basis. Basing sovereignty on a heterogeneous social base facilitates this soft determination of power. Power operates as an invisible presence and works best when undetected. Freedom is ignorance of the determining forces that regulate life. Within capitalism social limits and measures are consistently surpassed. Finding new creative mechanisms of expenditure, new ways to waste time, waste surplus wealth, this is the most important part of what appears as modern man's definition of 'progress' – more efficient ways to make waste. People are free so long as they know their place as consumers who depend on the market for their wages and sustenance.

With soft determinations of power certain transgressions are allowed, and therefore hold the potential of revolutionizing the multitude at the level of the thought. Certain mental illnesses, although not entirely glamorous and are extremely uncomfortable for the person experiencing those illnesses, also show what is possible at the level of sense. Rather than posing communist ontology as an equitable sort of distributive justice, it may be more constructive to start the revolution at the level of sense. There are many reasons to remain optimistic about this sort of change. Cooperation is in fact the living and productive pulsation of the multitude. One reason to stay optimistic is the simple realization that cooperation is key to survival. It is a clumsy man, still incapable of eluding the intrigues of nature, who locks being in the me. People can change their subjective relations.

In this way, there is power in the networks formed through the cooperation of labor. Power is not simply the property of the bourgeoisie. It circulates, like blood through a body, currency through an economy, or like electricity through channels on a grid. With the advanced network of communication technology that capital has produced, ideas travel at an infinite speed throughout the entire body politics. Through networks, relays, and flows of political discourse, the multitude can explore the infinite possibilities of liberation. Many a listless summer has already passed by in sight on the side of the road of life.

# HUMANS DOING, HUMANS BEING

HERE WE GO LABORING TO REMEMBER THE FORGOTTEN SUBJECT of our being. Have we forgotten to be? Can we remember what it is to Be? Being of being as being-beings. What is given as the real world is the world of production – today we must be doing, making, becoming beings. A world of creation awaits us in this very real and uniquely presence of the 'now' of historical actualization. Our present world is the actualization of historical thought-images and historical consciousness. There is no pure creation of the self, because there is some semblance of carryover from the past. There is no creation that is not also a production. This is not a Cartesian: "I produce therefore I am," that sort of mind body dualism is dead.

Union with the self-constituted motto: *production is being.* There is no being without production. Generation of the self is always a productive action. What tools do we have out of which to construct ourselves? A myriad of technological devices spring to mind and yet the most rudimentary, age-old, and time-tested tool humans must make ourselves is language. We use words to express thoughts, emotions, desires, and to engage in communication to bring joy into our lives through humor, to express our pains, to find bonds with others through friendships and love relationships.

Language is an indispensable tool with which to at the very least communicate in the hopes of obtaining some of the very real human wants and needs that can only be satisfied through social relations. Why would we need words and body language to communicate if we knew what everyone always wanted? Language becomes necessary because humans have no innate ability to read minds there is no psychic power (yet proven); and we do not have the power of telekinesis. So, something simple like sitting at a dinner table and asking the person across from you to please pass the salt, language becomes necessary in even the most ordinary day to day situations because the person across from me cannot read my mind and intuitively know that I want the salt at that exact moment.

In Buddhist circles, there is a common cliché, stop yourself from becoming a human doing and sit quietly as a human being. The rapid pace of modern life distracts us from the beauty of stillness. People are often capable of doing, making, and producing, but unable to communicate about the most basic things that they want and need at even the most fundamental day to day emotional and physical levels.

Far too many people live in the same house with other people, perhaps family members they have inhabited the same space next to for years and years, without taking the time to learn about these fascinating human beings. Like ships passing in the night we brush past the most important people in our lives without truly peeling away the outer shell of the hardened oyster to reveal the beauty of the glistening pearl that lay within, we must awaken the pearl and be mindful to cast these pearls towards those who are gracious enough to appreciate its beauty.

While meditating my dharma friend Wei-Bo always uses the gong method. This means he hits the gong and lets it stop. He hits it again and lets it stop. Over and over creating sound and then silence. Again, and again for half an hour until he quiets the gong with the palm of his hand. We sit and focus on the gong. He stops the gong from ringing with his hand

and always says: "Notice the silence. Be the silence within. Notice that the sounds happen around the silence."

For the slightest millisecond, there is a perfect stillness. It is a powerful practice to be at one with that moment of stillness. To be the still center of the wheel of life as well as the spokes that move. Be the hollow, empty, still center that stays put without being pulled by this or that new cultural fashion and know that the wheel turning is one with the still center. As an old zen saying goes: do not attach oneself to any dharmic flow. Improvement exists merely as a perception within the mind and all clinging of mind constitutes the source of suffering. With uncertainty and quietly in ambiguity, progress creeps forward, not knowing the full outcome of its effects. Eventually, what appears at first to be progress turns out to be a burdensome intrusion, a surplus.

The Buddha says time and time again in many different places: Form is Void, Void is Form. What he is really saying is that what is empty must remain empty. The mind is the form that contains thoughts, and the thoughts are the vessels that express intentions. To have virtuous intentions one must empty the mind of negative thoughts. The unhealthy thoughts are always ready to crop back in unless the intentions behind them are fundamentally transformed. Intentions cause thoughts. Thoughts cause actions. Every evil action in the world is the result of an evil thought, hatred, greed, selfishness, are all a result of the ego remaining in charge of human intentions. Go back to the source and the deeper you go the more you will have an awareness of the intentions.

The further into the mid one digs the more awareness the mind will bring to itself. In most philosophies of the mind there are textbook definitions of the mind and the brain. Usually they leave the ego completely out of the equation. The mind is usually defined as the actions in the brain. The brain is the physicality of the gray matter itself. It is a tangible object. When scientists study what parts of the brain perform certain functions, they can observe people who see color and people who are color-blind.

When people who see colors have a green light in front of their eyes it stimulates a region of the brain. Researchers at Harvard have pinpointed a small portion of the brain behind the temples near the back of the brain that lights up with activity when colorful objects are visible. In color-blind people, there is no stimulation in this part of the brain and therefore they do not see the colors. An old debate that will probably never be settled is whether the color is intrinsic to the object, or whether it is intrinsic to the brain. A well renowned analytical philosopher Ludwig Wittgenstein axiomatically posited the thesis that 'objects are colorless'; he is claiming that color is a mental construct in the brain. Mind-only consciousness rears its head yet again, and every perception of color, or literally anything else is all explained by the immanent workings of the mind in concert with the physical components of the brain. Can we ever really answer this fundamental question? Will it ever be resolved? Humans can see, touch, feel, perhaps even taste an object but we cannot truly know if the thing-in-itself, as it is, exists beyond our mere perception of it. In this way, the entire universe cannot truly be known beyond our sense of it, and therefore, it has been argued that all of existence is merely an idea in our mind. This is called idealism. No one can ever truly get to the other side of the horizon of one's own perception.

George Berkeley the idealist philosopher argued that all sensations are a product of the mind. His thesis was that there was no way to prove the existence of the world. All epistemological arguments concluding that have tried to prove the existence of objects outside of the mind must rely on sense experience to do so. Sense perceptions give us an idea of the object, but cannot tell someone conclusively whether the thing-in-itself exists.

The thing-in-itself is the existence of the object beyond our sense perception of it. This is often misunderstood by undergraduates as the thesis that the world disappears if there is no subject there to perceive it, which is about as solipsistic you can get in metaphysics. The absurdity of thinking that the whole universe is created and destroyed through the actions of a single mind seems a big metaphysical loophole justifying human existence.

Be it the mind of God, or the absolute mind constituting the sum of all human consciousness this thesis tends to appeal those with serious bravado, can we be forgiven for thinking we matter? Matter so much that the entire universe is fabricated at our whim? Or, is it more insane to think the entire universe was created as a figment borne out of the mind of a greater dreamer, a God-that-dreams? This always ties back to the ego and at a deeper level a substantial self. If we are Gods-image then Gods-mind created us and we create out of our minds and perhaps this is the essence of what it is to be an intentional, creating being.

In my experience the deeper and deeper one digs the more it becomes obvious that the self is un-thing-able. It cannot be objectified. There are intuitions and desires but no concrete self behind the scenes pulling the strings making it go. All of that is an edifice borne out of habit. The world forms the self itself. Moving in active intuition from the made to the making. Everything is being-made. Being is always being-made. Open to the possibility of becoming something other than what it currently is.

It is not a thought of intrinsic direct causality in the sense that something necessarily always happens because of a certain course of action. On the other hand, this movement catches everyone off guard. As Monty Python famously said: No one expects the Spanish Inquisition! It is production in the sense of directors saying: 'lights camera action' lose the script! Improvise! The world is but a stage; we are merely players, performers and portrayers. The contingency of chance events that produce unexpected results where events are Being an unexpected guest that arrives, gives a gift without expecting anything in return and dashes away.

Production as being that turns consciousness into a moving, doing entity that has stillness at the core of its essence.

Behaviors exhibited in daily life often become trance perspectives that frame consciousness in such a way that work becomes an almost inescapable trap.

Man, is a contradictory essence of freedom and necessity.

This is the ontological contradiction. What we are free to do is often not what is required of us to survive. Production is necessary to create the material goods required to sustain life, which requires labor, and that means, on some level, giving up our absolute freedom in order to transform raw materials into products and goods for consumption. We are always trying to overcome this metaphysical contradiction between what we want and what we must do. What we believe and the realities of what is. Ontology is about navigating the pathway between freedom and necessity. We both must and cannot think that in the world there is a beginning. And we are all free to escape into stories that make the day easier to get through, that make the work easier to do.

For instance, the belief that the world is nothing more than an idea in the mind, makes all the suffering and pain seem easier to handle. If the Buddha convinces us that the self does not exist, then there is no one there to feel the suffering that goes along with being in the world. There is suffering and it is caused by clinging of mind, a self that clings to the world, and the ways of the world, will always suffer, that is the basic fact of Buddhist teachings.

A Buddhist monk practicing a long deep meditative withdrawal began to feel the presence of a spider. Every day he meditated this spider appeared and mortified him, he could feel the spider crawling on his skin, growing larger and more menacing each time. Until finally it grew as big as the monk himself and appeared quite threatening.

After becoming weary with this presence day after day the monk finally asked his guru for advice. The guru said, "When you see the spider take a piece of chalk. Mark an X on the belly of the spider, and then take a very sharp knife and plunge it into the X." The monk convinced the guru to watch over him as he meditated. On the very next day, the monk began meditating and again the spider appeared. Crawling on his skin. The monk marked where the belly of the spider appeared with an X. He opened his eyes to see that the X was directly in the middle of his navel. As the guru saw the X and the monk retold him what happened to which the guru proclaimed: "I did not see a spider crawling on your skin. The spider you must vanquish lay within your own mind."

The contradiction comes in knowing what is thinkable, what we are free to think and conceive. What is necessary, what we must think and do to sustain ourselves and create ourselves. What fears we must unpack before we can move forward. What fears must be unpacked by moving forward.

Psychology has several terms for mind-only consciousness – narcissism, solipsism, monomaniacal, and so forth. People who believe in mind-only consciousness are always in pain. Mind-only consciousness is an escape from pain, because the hurt inside subjects the person to such immense anguish, the person obtains release by escaping from the pain of life. It is as if the suffering is so immense the only way to negate it is to deny the existence of the entire realm of existence as an actual thing-in-itself. If the cause of pain does not exist, then the pain also melts away. Openness means being vulnerable. Relationships also mean the risk of opening to pain. Despite the well-intentioned advice of others, emotional pain must be suffered alone.

Time as self-identity is continually moving from past to future. The "eternal now" is self-contradictory. Start with the world as it presents it-self. As it is and then gain access to the present as an active becoming, rather than seeing it as a stagnant dead end. Marx plays an influence in his work because Ideas are always produced from a relationship to the material world and mode of production-itself, not the other way around, yet people are not stamped out like the factories Blake so vehemently called the 'dark satanic mills' the ideas created by creators are created by the ingenuity of the human mind. It is easy to believe that the talents of general intellect can solve every problem and that the resources offered by the human mind are limitless. A savory temptation to put total trust in human genius.

The thing that the Heart and Diamond Sutras teach is that there is no self. Or, to put it another way, the self is an empty appearance. For some unknown reason this terrifies the Western Subject. There must be a reason why events happen. There must be a way to fix these problems. In fact, most of the serious political problems in the world are usually avoided until they reach the point of no return due to rationalizing away the urgency neces-sary to make the recommended changes. There is no shortage of scientists who have proven the increasing intensity of ecological problems due to over consumption of fossil fuels, and the ransacking of the planet to obtain them. Yet, the urgency necessary to compel international world wide glob-al action to save the planet seems to get rationalized away, probably out of denial that the problems are really this bad. Scholars document problem after problem and still nothing changes. Everything must be packed nicely away in their proper place and all actions must be reasonable, calculable, rational, and make sense. In looking around the world, there is very lit-tle that conforms to these guidelines in the artificial cultural milieu that surrounds us in Western Societies. Simulation is a temporary trap as the reality of the worlding-world creeps back into being as a presence. We have to go into the world to produce ourselves, now more than ever in modern society, we live our time. We are always stepping forth into time standing outside ourselves, throwing ourselves into life-projects, stretching into the future, and we either do this, or the time is lost, irrecoverably.

Deconstructing this perspective leads to the conclusion that history guides opinions, beliefs, discourses, and the over-arching ethos of every socially constructed episteme (truth-regime). However, at any given time there are people who serve as outliers who refuse to accept these constructs and make changes, but we hardly hear of these people.

Life is hard for these dissidents. In most of the despotic regimes on earth dissidents are cast aside as refugees, exiled, imprisoned, or murdered by the state for simply uttering words that cast aspersions about whether the person is loyal to the leader. It is a zero-sum game where life and limb are on the line. This means overcoming the fear of the nothing, and seeing the humor in the absurdity of existence. It is kind of sad that there is no discernible reason why life can be so tragic, but there is also a certain cosmic humor in knowing that it is completely temporary. The one truth about life, it goes on, until it doesn't go on.

As a Zen master was once asked why people should meditate. He answered: "It is important to do housecleaning from time to time." To clear out the junk that accumulates in the cluttered mind. To practice detachment and to unravel the ways that we cling to mind-noise. Many a listless summer has passed by without notice.

Wiping the slate clean to blossom like the lotus in reverence for the chain of life. A reverence for all life happens when there is a realization that nature takes thousands of years to perfect even the smallest wild flower. A flower that took a billion years to evolve into those beautiful blossoms and then folds over and dies with the changing season. This the awareness of the *continuity of discontinuity*. Everything is connected as if in an ontological continuum. There are flows and breaks in the flows to life. Connections and disconnections; attachments and detachments, and it is all temporary. It all goes away someday. A life is temporal. The forms are shaped by material conditions and evolutionary circumstances that have built up forms over the course of uncountable lifetimes. One life is a ripple in the movement of this sacred water that continues like a child facing out until reaching the boundless open sea.

# THE BOUNDLESS OPEN SEA: NIHILISM AND ETHICS

She should have died hereafter;
There would have been a time for such a word.
To-morrow, and to-morrow, and to-morrow,
Creeps in this petty pace from day to day
To the last syllable of recorded time,
And all our yesterdays have lighted fools
The way to dusty death. Out, out, brief candle!
Life's but a walking shadow, a poor player
That struts and frets his hour upon the stage
And then is heard no more: it is a tale
Told by an idiot, full of sound and fury,
Signifying nothing.
   - Macbeth


…perhaps there has never yet been such an 'open sea'.
   - Friedrich Nietzsche, The Gay Science

If God does not exist, then everything is permitted.
   - Fyodor Dostoevsky, The Brothers Karamazov

If God does exist, then everything is permitted.
   - Gilles Deleuze, Francis Bacon

W HEN FRIEDRICH NIETZSCHE ORIENTS HIMSELF TOWARDS THE foundationless thesis that God is Dead, he immediately writes, probably as a subconscious slip that we must now encounter the boundless open sea. An uncanny feeling that our morals are coming unglued. Emancipation from the authority of social institutions can be a frightening possibility for some. It means admitting the obvious fact that man is an animal that merely makes promises. A presupposition that has become ordinary in our time once felt to be the uncovering of infinite possibilities. Yet, his work may have unraveled the groundwork of western metaphysics prompting a despairing eternal return to the origins of western metaphysics. We have now unraveled the mysteries that God was created by Man in Man's image; and we see before us the shock and awe of the boundless open sea. Now, it is important to note that Thales and Anaximander are widely regarded as the first two purely Western Philosophers. Thales argued that water underpinned all of reality as the most important of the elements. He also argued that God existed in everything (an early Pantheist who posited the omnipresence of God). Trickle of time passing like drops of water through a river to the sea. To-morrow, to-morrow, to-morrow, pulling us ever forward, with or without our permission.

Anaximander hypothesized that existence was underpinned by the 'Boundless' the 'Infinite' or what he called the "Apeiron" which means right at the outset of Western Philosophy we have a Boundless Open Sea. The Death of God brings us back to the beginning; i.e. deconstructive progress. What have we created under the auspices of 'progress'?

What is ethics in a world dominated by war machines and profit motives? Can there be ethics at all in this kind of world? In my opinion, to have ethics is to change this entire world into relations that are hospitable.

The way of the world is the object that ethical critique resists. Nihilism acquiesces in the way of the world and takes a ruthlessly apathetic stance towards material, psychical, and social-political exigencies of great magnitude. The world is a network of relations and of occasional purposefulness where the obstacle is the path. Nihilism is the obstacle obstructing the path to a better tomorrow, but if we continue with ethics, it becomes nihilistic, if we plunge into nihilism it becomes obvious that nothingness can ground ethics (i.e. nothing, or *The Nothing* grounds ethics).

Perhaps what humans refer to as God is not in fact something that made human beings in His image, but the truth may be that humans in fact made God in theirs. Many social political philosophers have hypothesized this exact theory namely among them Emile Durkheim who believed that the concept of God was a sum total of human being's consciousness in their social relations.

Which in saying that God is a concept that amounts to the sum-total of actual social relations is not the same as giving a thesis of a hopeless nihilist. There is a sense that one can admire the academic ability to make Nietzsche seem like a bank manager, Bataille like an occupational therapist, or Derrida world-historic, but in the end, one vomits.

Probably the most recognizable phrase in all of Nietzsche is often misunderstood death of God, which is attributed to his nihilism. Yet, nihilism appears to have the effect of deconstructing any values and standards without a form of utopian gesture or renewal. It is an anti-ethos or rather the notion that there are no intrinsic values in the universe, and specifically no ethical values, except for those that humans create as fictions. Beware of those who do battle with monsters, for they will become monsters themselves.

Metaphysics is a soft lullaby to soothe latent existential anxieties, a cry of an oppressed people yearning for another life because the suffering in this one has become overwhelming, and religion enables stubborn beings to remain in ethical stasis, unable to think freely. All we have are echoes of our own mind. Religion creates reactive slaves when life is a tale told by an idiot with much sound and fury, signifying nothing. Values are lies that harden into truths over time, or as Nietzsche claims 'truth is an illusion we have forgotten is such' the well-worn coins completely effaced to be little more than metal tokens containing no a-priori value. There is a subtle difference between what one might call proper or ethical critique and nihilism. One subtle distinction is that nihilist critique that ends in a negation and ethics ending in a positive assertion of utopian values. The peculiarity is that ethics tries to resolve itself in a way that will somehow improve material conditions: emotional, spiritual, physical, or even intangible. Nihilism on the other hand critiques with the intention of revealing the depravity of these conditions without any hope of improving them. Nihilism paved the way for Jacques Derrida. Deconstruction is about irresolvable problems and intractable contradictions that reveal entanglements posed by the way languages construct "the Truth" (i.e. truth on a meta-physical level). Resolutions are impossible and this lends itself to a nihilistic antithetical and hopeless perspective on ethical issues. Deconstruction is the open-denouement of nihilism.

For instance, saving lives, prolonging lives, and ameliorating poverty seem like noble ethical goals, but it leads to overpopulation and sucking up irretrievable resources. Consumption levels and overpopulation has become such a problem that if the two largest countries in the world, India and China, maintain their current course of industrial development to consume at the same levels as the United States of America, the earth must produce twelve times the natural resources to sustain life at that level of materialism. Lower gas prices lead to over consumption of oil which pollutes the air and causes global warming. Using gas also diminishes the natural reserves of oil which will eventually run out completely.

Sustaining and prolonging lives, especially in so-called 'developed countries' also leads to greater stress on food supplies which puts a strain on natural eco-systems and animals. So ethics and nihilism can dovetail off each other to the point where someone seeking an ethical lifestyle must either live with complete blinders on, ignorant about the impact his or her consumption patterns have on the long-term strength of the planet, or live a completely ascetic lifestyle along the lines of that espoused by Simone Weil whose ethical positions involved a complete rebuking of any material indulgences, even particular kinds of food, or clothing, or using technology that would compromise her position that she would find solidarity with the least among us by only experience what they experienced. Her moral asceticism was meant as a commitment to total self-sacrifice, not to bring about greater self-expression, but rather as a way of minimizing harm.

In my opinion, Simone Weil has an utterly convincing thesis on the need for ethical grounding, yet her asceticism lead to her ultimate demise and the hunger strike resulting in her suicide, because in acting in solidarity with the oppressed, by taking a Bodhisattva vow to end others suffering, even to the point of denying her own path to Nirvana, she in fact, added to the suffering in the world by compounding it immanently within herself. Her nihilism was almost like the early Buddha in the extreme denial of the body to the point of self-inflicted violence, which calls to mind the religious practice of being penitent to God by performing self-flagellation, literally whipping or beating the body, to cause suffering as a cleansing process, catharsis for guilt and shame for a living a life of sin. Sin being the joy that comes from giving into temptations and experiencing pleasure in something forbidden like sex, or foods, or otherwise betraying the "Word" or "Logos" of God. As you can see the division between ethical critique and nihilism is extremely blurry. Both increase suffering. The first noble truth reads: "There is suffering"; it is inextricable with existence. Nature is based on suffering. The lion must eat a gazelle to survive, the gazelle is there to suffer and die, to keep the chain of being alive by giving up its life – yet, one must question the perfection of such a system that relies so heavily on violence to maintain this chain of life. Euthanizing the weakest links to maintain the strongest seems unfair to those born simply to be disposed among the weak. Predators and prey are a part of existence in the animal kingdom, however, humans are vibrantly aware of our suffering. Cursed by awareness the sense of our suffering compounds and prolongs the it through the echo-chamber that is the resonance of memory. Ethics and compassion may amount to nothing more than active-forgetting and active-suppression.

To my knowledge deconstruction is a radical anti-methodological methodology intended to strip away false consciousness without any intended result and to reveal the dead end of being, texts, and socio-political orders.

De-constructing removes these obstacles to move past what was previous though to be impassable. The sole intention is to reveal that there are no transcendental a-priori absolutes underpinning ethics or politics; but to still move forward, keeping a sense of self, which means that if a being completely erases a sense of progress then that being loses all sense of striving, and loses the sense of fulfillment that comes from accomplishing something one has set out to accomplish. The purpose or lack of purpose was to breakdown to create anew and certainly not wanton destruction out of sadistic glee while beholding the suffering of others. Taking apart so as to perhaps open the suture of an emotional trauma-wound but just long enough to let the emotional demons escape and not so long that one picks at it obsessively thereby destroying any forward progress in life-movement.

Deconstruction cannot necessarily be reduced to a simplistic definition and in fact all attempts to place it within a lexical set of categories; a response to Heidegger, or literary criticism used to interpret ambiguity in texts, even juxtaposing Derrida with Levinas to create deconstructive ethics, in my opinion have fallen short of describing what makes it so poignant. The purpose of this text is not to describe deconstruction or to build a better mousetrap so to speak whereby old ideas are improved upon but rather to see if there is an ambiguity between nihilism and ethical critique whereby particular methodologies (which may or may not be methodical at all) can teach us about the problems inherent in ethical agency. Hundreds of years from now resources may be so scarce that life will be unsustainable and the way humans are ripping through the earth's bounty it could happen sooner rather than later.

As R.D. Laing once said to paraphrase, perhaps hundreds of years from now humans will look back at the way the mad are treated in our times and view it as completely barbaric. Leaving aside that this implies a naturally progressive evolution to human consciousness there is a point that needs to be addressed in that statement. Does civilization move ever so slightly towards an ever more perfect ethical situation? Do problems that seem to be intractable in our times eventually become transcended in future epochs, or is it closer to what Foucault posits, that each temporal episteme carries its own set of contradictions and a-priori social principles that, although they somewhat tie in with the previous episteme, it becomes utterly impossible to view history in a progressive, evolutionary paradigm. There is no forward progress but only a series of new problems and power relations that place some populations in the margins and others in positions of being on top of the historical dust heap. Times change and tops become bottoms, bottoms become tops, but no social order is closer or further to perfection, and even the visions of a perfectible society can be nightmarish. The point is that suffering is an obstinate part of life in this world. No person can seclude himself and believe the suffering will completely vanish.

The borderline between nihilism and ethical critique is ambiguous at best and at worst the distinction becomes completely effaced. True philosophical reflection involves un-tethering thought from the past and remaining open to genuine self-reflection, by remaining open to the possibilities of the future.

Heidegger did say that his thoughts were to 'take a hammer to metaphysics' as a tool-based liberation by reworking the violence inherent in the Onto-Theo-Logical edifice that has captured and entrapped philosophy. Once you de-struct metaphysics inherent in the Onto-Theo-Logical tradition and reveal the nothing, once the existential dread and anxiety have abated, the main project of philosophy becomes to create new concepts and edifices. Rather than bemoan the death of philosophy one can make philosophy concerned with, as some have called "fabulation", and creation which will make the world otherwise than it is. Critique at its core is about exposing errors, omissions, and falsehoods, deliberate or inadvertently held as truth claims. Ethical critique is an attempt to fix or resolve, not just contradictions in a given social system, but errors and faulty truth claims. Whether or not this is possible on any meta-social level is something I am skeptical about and this is what leads some people to become nihilistic and hopeless, the belief that there will always be some imperfection in any given social arrangement. Some oppression may always exist, but to go to the place where postmodernists like Foucault have tread is to almost admit that the path to liberation is itself poisoned with the illogic and faulty truth claims of the previous epistemological order that oppressed populations and will continue to oppress through subsequent organizations of power relations.

The world appears to be an inescapable prison or asylum that is until one looks inward to find that the whole thing is a complete fabrication made up by faulty representations of a misguided ego that convinced the subject it exists. The problem is not that the self is being oppressed or not being oppressed, but rather that the self has the ego convinced that it exists, when in fact, it does not. This was why Foucault was so provocative but ultimately failed to find an outside to the power dynamics he meticulously studied, because he did hallucinogenic drugs but never meditated. Had he turned to the East and looked inward he might have found the solution rather quickly, that the ego, the self, is not only interpolated by social constructs that call it as an individual (ala Louis Althusser), but rather individuals are interpolated in that one believes subjectivity is a thing that is actual rather than virtual, or that it must refer to a perceptible, knowable object.

In my honest opinion, this deconstructive ethos has been misused and watered down by cultural and moral relativists who abuse this ungrounded ethics to the point where oppressions that are clearly evil are dismissed as rhetorical word games because evil is believed to be a matter of perspective. This is the ethical conundrum in critical theory that is most bothersome in my opinion because if one takes away the ethical ground one must ultimately become a nihilist, there is no such thing as an affirmative criticism because by the very nature of being critical one negates. Even negative dialectics posit a negation as the affirmation that leads to a psychological discord in the subject a double bind, or cognitive dissonance will occur with the subject becoming utterly confused.

Husserl and Kant were correct in asserting that consciousness must maintain a sense of cognitive unity through the active synthesis of the intuitive manifold occurring a-priori in what I will call the "pre-rational subject", or what Deleuze may have had in mind when he used the term the "larval subject" in *Difference and Repetition*. A not yet fully formed subject who acts solely on intuition will find that their ethics will be ungrounded and changeable over time due to varying circumstances and conditions. In fact, Sartre writes in the Transcendence of the Ego that intuitions if they go un-checked will ultimately tie the subject in knots by posing interminable contradictions, which make any ethical or active self utterly impossible. The schizo-subject cannot stay schizzed forever and even Deleuze and Guattari realized this by claiming at the end of *A Thousand Plateaus* that de-territorialization always co-relates back to re-territorialization. What I take this to mean is that the defragmenting of the mind must always resolve back into a transcendental synthesis to maintain its continuity in space, time, and ultimately in ethical agency as well. Otherwise the subject becomes self-alienated and nihilistic.

Can there be a way to look inward without becoming alienated and the answer is ambiguous – once self-reflection occurs it becomes obvious that the 'me' beyond the self is nothing, or creating out of nothing. In fact, the dilemma that the snuggling hedgehogs face is not only about social interactions with an external Other. The example is also about an immanent relation to the self. The close one gets to the self within the more hostile one may become. Inward hostility on a cold winter night as the hedgehogs grow closer they poke each other with their spines and as they draw further away they grow colder. It is the yin and yang of the self, which one cannot truly know without arduous effort, and even then, it is a con game because the self is an illusion. The self becomes an impersonal singularity, a non-being.

TRANSCENDENTAL SYNTHESIS revolves around consciousness coming into unity with itself. The a-priori intuition of time and space are manifold in nature meaning they are at first heterogeneous, disparate, and lacking in continuity. As we age and gain experience this manifold becomes synthesized into a whole subject, but only through its epistemological experience of an external object. Through striving to know about the external world the manifold intuitions can be overcome to create rational thinking and knowing subjects. With a subject, there is an object. To think means to think about something. But, this is not always the case. There are subjects who think in a totally detached manner void of any object, and this is psychosis. It also occurs in meditations that take on nothingness as an object to ponder. Literally emptying the mind can liberate it from itself by ameliorating clutter and useless thoughts. Critique must begin with this step-to maintain an ethical perspective. To become too attached to a social discourse is to remain in the realm of an obstructed view of the object in question.

For instance, Foucault tells us quite eloquently that there are 'transversal' modes of oppression. That is there are oppressions that transcend economic, social, and political formations like the oppression of the mad, or children, or criminals, or students, or the poor. Basically, one cannot pinpoint a socio-economic formation like capitalism, or patriarchy, or theocracy that create these oppressions, rather they exist within social orders that never fell under these categories. Taking a position that one must ameliorate a kind of exploitation or power relation means that one is limiting the modus operandi of one's efforts towards liberation. One is doomed to fail if One acts like a lone hero in solitude. An atomized individual is destined to fall flat when acting in complete isolation; and yet there are all these stories of superhuman will power where people transform systems through sheer force of individual will and desire. A common dyad is the forced non-choice between individual 'no one will understand' and 'you cannot succeed alone' when in fact these are two sides of the same coin. Economic exploitation is not merely a capitalist experience, but could be a human being experience, and this is the biggest obstacle to ethical critique which reforms itself into a nihilistic abyss, where one says, there is no hope. The problems appear to be far too massive to be completely fixed and therefore what is the use in even thinking about these exigencies.

Transcendental consciousness cuts through the subject like a blade and clears out the ambiguity by making itself consciousness of an empirical object. The opaqueness of the subject in its manifold intuitive a-priori states are clarified by the experiential unity which unfolds as the transcendental subject passes through time-space and plumbs the depths of the unknown. Projecting outwards into the abyss mirrors the process of inward self-reflection that binds the subject to a pre-conscious transcendental field, a cosmic metaphysical oneness that precludes the realm of mere objects. It is where we came from and it is where we return upon death. As Lao Tzu says, there is a force older than God, it is called the Tao. This is sense of chi, oneness, or balanced harmony is what the transcendental consciousness strives towards in its unity between the self, the world, and the cosmos. All meta-discourses play on this mythos, or this striving to reunite the fallen subject with something greater than itself, a community, a God, a nation, a transcendental ideal of anOTher that may or may not actually exist.

These pose massive hallucinatory projections that distort History and its forward progress. Objectless-subjects backslide into phantasies and un-resolved conflicts burdened from this pre-conscious transcendental field that saturates the way material conditions are represented, and re-collected back to the subject in an echo-chamber inwardly reflecting upon emptiness or what some Buddhists call Sunyata, where emptiness is form, and form is empty. Or, rather a Satori moment when the heavens open and cosmi-cally all the blocks in the skyward castle known as metaphysics crumble to the ground, only to be revealed in the sand beneath ones toes as we walk barefoot on a tropical beach holding hands, solely alone, bonded by the unity-mind and loving-kindness that emits warmness rising out of the center that is there, but not there, within you, me, and every being that has ever existed. The form becomes non-form. Fullness becomes emptiness.

Life becomes death and death returns in another cosmic form bouncing back again and again until there is no-thing at all. Just pure spirit, and in our nihilistic, post-modern malaise we are unable to see this because we fail to see the rationale behind irrationality when our spirit is so repressed, when existence (or as Heidegger calls it – ontology, the being of beings) is a paradox that was never meant to be solved. Existence was meant to be enjoyed and suffered. Good is what is good to the desire of the subject. All we have are echo chambers of our own mind and yet we accomplish communication. It is a riddle.

We are meant to live in the neither and both. The negation that affirms and the rigidity that leads to resistance, because it creates things that ultimately break, erode, and die. Like the body that grows feeble. Nihilism posits the feeble hopelessness of death it makes the eschaton immanent, and focuses on death before life is over. Ethical critique provides ambient life that cogently reorganizes the truth that is underneath the misguided or ideological subject (and who can talk politics or religion without being zapped instantly by ideology). It is anti-ideological to remain open to the unknown. To realize we do not know a-priori what answers are coming, what questions may have no answers, and what cosmic mysteries will remain permanently unsolvable. But to still engage with the questioning, not as an interrogation, or as a trivia challenge, but as someone who would rather carve out a space to posit unique subjectivities beyond the masses with their homogeneous final solutions.

"Today we consider it a matter of decency not to wish to see everything naked, or to be present at everything…One should have more respect for the bashfulness with which nature has hidden behind riddles and multiple uncertainties. Perhaps nature is a woman who has reasons for not letting us see her reasons?" And if we take Nietzsche seriously, this quote from the first portions of the Joyful Science his point is that critique is not the elimination of errors, but rather, truth is a kind of error. A deviation that allows the individual to avoid losing its sense of selfhood en masse. Illusions are inherent in the way truth is formulated, meditated upon, and solidified into fact. Solidification is the error; the truth is in the breakdown of the solid because when "the Truth" melts into air it sustains the breath of life in inaccuracies and opens a space for existential universes and fictional world building (i.e. the imagination breaks free of the ground). When power is at its most rigid and inflexible the subjugated subject is bound to break free because resistance usually emerges at that point. It is precisely because the oppression becomes visible and unavoidable. Power that is invisible or unseen can sometimes linger on eternally and that is where 'the Truth' as solidity transmutes into another form – liquidation, or as is often the case, an ethereal escape from material entrapment and the engrossment of consumption.

A central component of Foucault's work on discourses is that they not only direct politics, but also actually constitute subjects externally and internally on a micro-political level. Subjects are constrained and disciplined by power, and yet the power often remains hidden, even while it enacts subjects into being. Our daily social life involves shaping bodies and mind. A point that is often overlooked in Foucault studies because of his famous line in *Discipline and Punish* that disciplinary power operates at the level of 'dressage' or the bodily form. On the other hand, I would argue there is ample evidence that disciplinary power also operates by correcting behaviors and mental configurations as well. Disciplinary power creates the conditions for its own deviance, which it then views as threatening. Foucault had in mind certain kinds of subjectivity – the "abnormals" (i.e. the mad, the criminal, the marginal, homosexuals, and differently gendered bodies tossed aside by humanism because they are allegedly monstrous).

Foucault proposed three defining features of disciplinary power in its early historical formations at around the time of the Enlightenment. First, hierarchical observation is "an apparatus in which the techniques that make it possible to see induced effects of power, and in which, conversely, the means of coercion make those on whom they are applied clearly visible." The increasingly precise surveillance that was a product both of a novel architecture organized around institutional functions, and new types of mutual scrutiny between members of institutions it facilitated, allowed disciplinary power to become an integrated system in which power functions anonymously and no longer requires overt force to have its effects.

Second, normalizing judgment was enacted through the micromanagement of behavior areas of social life from which penalty had been previously absent. Although in the mental hospital there are explicit regulations, the order imposed through discipline is of a further order: it legislates "natural and observable processes" to ensure greater conformity to a norm. For this reason, punishment is not only retaliatory but also corrective.[11] Disciplinary power also functions through reward, making it possible to define behavior as falling along a spectrum of "good and bad." "Through this micro-economy of a perpetual penalty operates a differentiation that is not one of acts, but of individuals themselves, of their nature, their potentialities, their level or their value."[12] This process of disciplinary power creates internally defined systems of meaning which are key to what Foucault would call, "normalization." It generates both a hierarchy and a set of punishments and rewards that can be used to manipulate individuals within the hierarchy to ensure greater homogeneity.

The third technique of disciplinary power is the examination. In ritualized forms of examination techniques incorporate the normalizing gaze as a mechanism of differentiation and evaluation. This technique gained ascendancy in the late 1700's and fundamentally shifted the discourse of human sciences toward the development of knowledge through the exercise of power in these sub- populations. Disciplinary power is invisible yet renders its subjects hyper-visible in order to tighten its grip: "It is the fact of constantly being seen, of being able always to be seen, that maintains the disciplined individual in his subjection."

Disciplinary power puts a why on a here that is no why. Humans all ask why and ponder existence, but metaphysics is inexplicable. Reality is here one minute and gone the next. As Quentin Meillasoux has recently postulated in his proposal that disturbs post-Kantian metaphysics, his theory of the 'arche-fossil'. A fossil is a material bearing the traces of pre-historic life, and by empirical observation of fossils, through carbon dating, we can estimate that dinosaur bones are approximately X-million or X-billion years old. Radioactive isotope decomposition provides an index as to the age of rocks and bones. Scientists can even provide the age of distant stars by indexing the luminescence of light coming off of them. Based on empirical observation of fossils, and objects, natural science estimates that the universe is roughly 13.7 billion years old, that the earth formed roughly 4.5 billion years ago, and that human ancestors originated about 2 million years ago, and that homo sapiens coming into existence a mere 100,000 years ago. It is no wonder we have so many ethical problems yet unresolved, humans have yet to figure out how to live life. Humans are predominantly violent because human life is in its infancy. The impulse is to make sense and figure out why, when in actuality, the mantra the universe exudes is "I don't know" – the moral discipline of higher consciousness (adhisilasikkhâ). In nihilism, "life takes on a value of nil."[1] Every value fades into nothing, and the experience of living becomes little more than a hazy fog with the subject trapped in illusions. The temptation of immortality constructs one such illusion, because it devalues this world in exchange

1 Gilles Deleuze. Nietzsche and Philosophy. Translated by Hugh Tomlinson. Pg. 147.

for an afterlife, which allegedly makes what is right in front of us in this actual world pale in comparison. Immortality depreciates life in the world of here and now.

The problem with immortality is that it takes the tragedy out of death. If we are immortal then we lose our deaths, we live our death and die our lives (as Sartre says) – a Buddhist Koan. As Jean Francois Lyotard points out a differend is when two or more parties have valid points but the legitimacy of one countervailing argument does not negate the legitimacy of the opposite position. There can be more than two legitimate positions on a particular topic and on an issue as wide ranging as metaphysics there are infinite postulations that can be held as true, more or less it is a matter of which fictions feel right and comfortable rather than which ones are empirically provable as "the Truth" (meta-physical allegations, or truth from above). Possessing the truth or being possessed by it as in some mystical experience means a radiating sense that comes with a feeling of security. Metaphysical truths when they are transcendental and synthetic fuse together antithetical positions, but the telos of this epistemological project is to ward off anxiety and hopelessness in a kind of epic-hero-making process. As we write navigate the abyss and construct the poems of our lives we attempt to ward of despair and nihilism through metaphors and the immortal epic narrative that is our life in its day to day unfolding, which culminates in nothing, and has no intrinsic purpose outside of the meanings we create for ourselves.

If there is a super-ego or a transcendental conscience that talks to us through interpolating voices, beckoning us to remain moral, then it echoes sonic communication apparatuses surrounding the subject, subsuming it and becoming its most intimate psychical mind-thoughts. Our higher self mirrors our social self and is always burdened with desiring-productions

that produce without creating value external to the subject itself. A self-re-
ferring matrix compounds suffering, as we will see in the next chapter. A
mind that echoes itself, which is actually all we have, leave little room to
learn, and expand its horizons with new experiences, and new knowledge.
But, is there a mind-independent world, or all we all reverberating the
same clichés back to us, appropriating, unable to gain new knowledge?

# Mysteries of Existence

E XISTENCE, OR WHAT PASSES AS EXISTENCE, IS A BRIEF INTERLUDE with a shadow. Science may put a semblance of a verifiable set of clothes on this passing shadow. Young children know that the shadow of existence has no clothes. Human life has become exhausted laboring under the illusion of self-imposed responsibility to be the sole reason for the universe to exist. Different from grasping, the gesture of greeting enables openness between the subject and object. Greeting is an invitation to that which lays within. Meditation is a gaze within that provides an already useful energy to thought and this is because there is a strange placebo effect underlying every transformative experience. To have a radical transformative experience in deep-meditation one must already halfway believe in the power of meditation. If it is the belief in the transformative experience that creates the effect of the transformative experience, then the question becomes, why engage in the transformative experience at all? Wouldn't the belief in change be enough to be the transformative experience itself?

Well, therein lies the rub. Meditation is not an action in the sense of material bodies crashing into one another, meditation is an action in non-corporeal, intangible, shifts in intention that then create new ripples of consciousness. Action means sitting perfectly still in a body in its physical form and transforming the intentions inherent in the void of the mind.

Void giving rise to all life and therefore void is fundamentally evolutionary in its nature.

The function of the gaze within is that it always already originates from a subject in possession of a willingness to look within. This is willful suspension of disbelief is what I call the enigma of existence. Buddha gazes and meditates, wistfully sitting, open to existence as it is. In the realization that nowhere is anything lasting, phenomena appear, exist, and then disappear; gone forever, existing only to those brave enough to circumnavigate the tumultuous caverns of memory. The decrepitude of the material realm, the impermanence of the body, is an invariable form of variation a kind trick played by the gods upon those with a strange fascination with repetition of the same in all its various guises.

The trick of the mind is to view the isness as stasis, but even stasis is becoming static. One sleight of hand trick that the mind plays on the brain and body is to concede all control of itself to the desire tending towards as little exertion of energy as possible, a constant temptation in a technologically subsumed carcass of a society that dissolves will power into the comfortable numbness of sofa-narco-terrorism, computer-coma, and infotainment-soma. All existence is becoming. We become our ways out of what was once comfortable in personal relationships. Even sitting still is becoming stillness. Emptying the mind opens it up to resonances, pulses, power-flows, and integral dynamics with itself and the external world, these fanatical intrusions into our lives unsettle the concrete reality that we are mind-brains sealed off in our own bodies – only alone.

Minds never fully rest until death. Minds are like tribes, diverse populations, worlds unto themselves. Talking impersonally to know itself in a hybrid sense. Even in nocturnal slumbers there is movement and action. The mind reflects the chaos and flux in the world that it observes. Our life is like a dream, it is not actually a dream, because stating that it is anything at all would mean life becomes a factual object about which one can state a concrete sense of reality. In our better hours, we wake up just enough to realize that we are dreaming. Shining light in the room means gradually peeling away more and more layers of knowledge, ceding that we start life seeking curiously perhaps even with hubris in our adolescence. Beginning from a position of not knowing our status of not knowing, rather than knowing, which means the not knowing our not knowing gives a false sense of certainty, which is much more terrifying than simply admitting we do not know, because that would imply we know we do not know.

There is nowhere anything lasting, neither outside me, nor within me, but only incessant change. I nowhere know of any being not even my own. There is no being. I myself know nothing and am nothing. There are only images: they are the only things which exists, and they know of themselves in the manner of images…I myself am only one of these images. All reality is transformed into a wondrous dream, without a life which is dreamed about, and without a spirit which dreams; into dream which coheres in a dream of itself.

To awaken consciousness is to slip into the gossamer phantasms of a dream-state. The Buddha, the awakened one, was aware because he knew this Suchness and saw reality as an illusory transitional point. An eternity opposed to permanence, that which is desirable precisely because it is unattainable in every respect, repetition is a transgression. It puts law into question, it denounces the nominal or general character in favor of more profound artistic reality. Once the love-desired-object is in our possession it always fails to meet our expectations. The inevitable rust of time sets in as one becomes comfortable with the presence of the Other, welcoming it into the wholeness of what one is, melting its difference into the background of our daily lives.

Extra-ordinary becoming merely ordinary, and the paranoia of being beside oneself being fused into a placated boredom with what one merely is. Surplus enjoyment seems like a surplus to those who lack in it, once the subject has that which was once viewed as a surplus, then it no longer seems surplus, the surplus of anOther becomes simply the ordinary way of life when the surplus falls into the possession of the Self. The play of life is an artistic creation that unfolds with each passing moment. Grasping the experience of now, tighter and tighter, is like trying to compress a handful of sand. The firmer the grip the faster the sand slips through the subject's fingers. Sitting with an open hand (and an open mind) means one can view the suchness, and cup the sand, to gently become aware of the moment as it passes. Unclenching the hand's grasp allows for the object to become stable within the subject's palm, but opening the hand, means that the sand still falls out and drifts away. The impermanence of this moment is like the hand holding sand. Everything is impermanent.

You never step twice into the same river, or the same capitalism, or the same self, precisely because the perception of what is perceived does not exhaust the possibilities of the perceptible. Certain zones of perceptions are accepted in the range of what appears and then there are myriads of other perceptible objects that simply do not register with consciousness as existing actual objects simply because these do not appear before the mind, these are the empty realms of the five skandhas; that which is there but simply does not register within the realm of the five senses. Much that is void contains something but may not appear and so seems empty, and it may very well be empty, to those who cannot see, this realm is virtual to them. To those who can see this is no longer empty because the light shone upon the darkness of the void and gave it form, therefore, the void is no longer merely a virtual possibility, the void is actual.

There are intentions and intent, and changing these subjective positions changes actions and agency. There can be no mindful action without intent. Actions without intent constitute the actions conducted under the fog of madness. Intent without contemplation is unguided intent and therefore cannot reach its goal, perhaps because it acts without a well-defined goal. No unintended actions exist and there are no unintentional agents when one uses mindfulness, but what surely exists are the misguided, untrained minds that have yet to become fully aware of how to contemplate (or of what is contemplated).

The untrained situation finds mindfulness to be second-guessing. The training one engages with in undergoing meditation practice leads to the realization that the self does not exist. The self is something other than the ego. As the Buddha says in the Diamond Sutra: there are no beings to be liberated. Having the awareness that one is a being means one will suffer. Where there is a self there is suffering (dukha).

It would seem merely perverse to believe that grasping after consciousness (vijnana) is one of the five ways of bringing suffering (dukha) down upon the subject, and that to lull consciousness to sleep is to find awareness (sati), but this is the paradox of the enigma of being. It would seem like an illusion to think that consciousness is linked (nidana) to the twelve-fold chain of contingent becoming (bhava-chakra). Yet, this is precisely the condition of possibility that is outlined by the rhizomatic-be comings that are a possibility, not a guarantee. When one link in the chain breaks, all the links break. The overcoming of ignorance and suffering leads to the elimination of consciousness, and the penultimate awareness that it does not exist in any substantial tangible manner. Residually, the traces of the ego vanish in nirvana and enlightenment. To put forth an "I" that exists is to make an order out of the Absurd. Order is an escape valve in an inauthentic machinic being-in-the-world an automata (a rhizome), a relation to oneself and the world that revises from recursive self-enhancement into automatic responsiveness and thus arrives at an entirely different state of the unconscious.

Reflexive living that posits the affirmative emptiness of the unknown in the subconscious, life in the present, whereby the subject has short term ideas. The incorporeal transformations of different events through temporal transitions in the material realm constitute the limit of consciousness. Without experiencing those flows the ego ceases to hold sway over the mind, and thus liberation occurs through detachment from the Oughtness of the is; to see reality in its Isness. Void is form and form is void, Is-ness without existence means to be without being. Interiority folded inward that extends to the outside, but still and detached from the stimuli of the world. As Deleuze says, "Repetition changes nothing in the object repeated, but does change something in the mind which contemplates it, the mind changes and the thing stays the same. What changes in the mind? Simply put, the mind finds the clarity with which to see the thing objectively as a thing-in-itself. If you see a flag waving on a brisk windy afternoon you might wonder. What is waving? The flag? The wind? Or, the mind? If mind detaches from object and only sees the repetitions as they occur in their sameness, then this position will stifle creative changes in the subject. Recurrences that are different, yet similar, create memories and re-collections that re-present (repeat the present) in a similar variation on an old theme. What is a habit? Perhaps we can claim that it is an attachment to desires that have become repetitious in passing through the five senses (skandhas). Settling the waters in the mind one can see the stillness even in the moving flag on a windy day.

The existence of the self depends upon the five skandhas (sight, sound, taste, touch, smell) which are empty. Consciousness is merely a bundle of memories, experiences, habits, emotions, and learned behaviors. Once behavioral momentum begins it becomes harder and harder to break a destructive habit than it is to never engage in destructive habits in the first place. Pride of knowledge in its purest flight always finds man eventually crashing back to earth falling face down in the mud. The skandhas provide a convincing, but ultimately virtual experience. If the skandhas, which are bundles of all these things wrapped together into an ego that thinks it exists, are taken apart piece by piece, then it will unravel the appearance that it is an immobile, unchanging object. Therefore, the body without organs is a composite of fragmentary perceptions assembled together through the skandhas. Taken apart we are what entrances our ephemeral skin.

Skandhas of men and women are differently oriented. The ephemeral skin that makes one egg a month has different priorities than the libidinal economics of desire structured as a perpetually-churning factory. To deny that there are forms to human gender is to relegate the conversation to saying that the concrete differences between people amount to nothing more than spit. What is fiction? A winter jacket put on a diary? Science puts a mathematical jacket on what anyone else calls plain sight. Perhaps because politics is dominated by money every four years America has erection results, and nothing that takes commitment gets done, because we are shooting off rockets into space rather than planting seeds for harvest. All vegetation uniformly grows towards the sun (except perhaps moss or some other fungi and mushroom formations that grow in the dark). Humans despite their treelike nature are still averting their eyes from the hidden secrets of nature.

Egolessness may mean that if the self is flexible, then it may also become non-phenomenal, transitional, slipping away from itself in total erasure. The irony is that to become aware of the becoming one must sit still and simply be. It may seem strange that immobility brings the self into greater flexibility. Being brings awareness of the becoming. Sound is in between the silence that radiates the resonance of what exists within. A purring cat tells you that the cat is experiencing joy, security, and perhaps a bond with the loving affectionate touch of a hand caressing its back and stroking its tail. Does every cat purr? Was the joy of security always already there within the cat? Or did the caress awaken these feelings through the loving touch that entrances a sensation within the feline?

Absurdity is awareness of existence in its emptiness. It is absurd because of the humor that arises when the full realization sets in that nothing is. The task of a bodhisattva is to liberate this interior illumination to pop the bubble, releasing the luster within self. The smallness of humility within the mind releases the meta-love that burgeons forth from beneath the surface. The enigma of the being of beings being. In the Buddhist sense, there is nothing instead of something, and something is the illusion. What exists need not be the way that it is, ripe-full of beautiful differences. If we were all the same the world would be quite a boring place. One time I mentioned this to a woman in a retail shopping center and she replied, "Yes, but we are all made in God's image. Beware because Jesus is coming, soon!" Which tells you the level of enlightenment at which many creatures operate on this planet, perhaps it is wrong to call these creatures 'human' because people who claim a pantheist-omniscience-omnipresence that replicates their beliefs, constructed out of their own personal ego, then this is not showing any sense of human-compassion.

There is one song. One verse - Uni-verse. Many refrains. Playing a song may involve playing chords which resonate many notes. Wines have many flavor notes. Wines are spirits. Sense in the world is that there is no carefully placed order from a transcendent divine Being. If I carefully observe every now and then I glimpse these ever-recurring flows. Universes are flows coming into unity with itself, returning from unity, spread to separation, gravitating back to unity. There are nomadic distributions and crowned anarchies. Everything is not equal and not everything returns, certainly not equally. Yet there is a refrain that somehow overlooks the differences.

A single and same voice for the whole thousand-voiced multiple, a single and same Ocean for all the drops, a single noise to being.

Unifying desire to be equal among all living beings, and the brute reality that things are out of place in the 'clamor of Being' and 'crowned anarchies' that push and pull the subject in an infinity of different directions, clouding the silence that the subject truly desires. Equality is difference. Beings are equal in their essential difference, rather than their essential sameness and unity is a result of seeing these fundamental differences and overcoming them to remain unified on a singular set of principles that produce joy. If the clamor of being brings a drop into the Ocean, then meditation is a bottle thrown into the boundless open sea, but without desperation, without ultimate verba, (one word to unify them all!) without its launch being a last attempt to signal and communicate a message entrusted with it. Since it is communicable, the transmutability of the phantasm leads to the nothingness of being, and what Nietzsche called nihilistic decadence.

Cultural decadence and cultural amnesia lead to every moment being fresh. The Buddhist dialectic is rooted in naivete. Mountains are mountains; water is water.

Thirty years ago, before I began the study of Zen, I said, 'mountains are mountains, waters are waters.' After I got an insight into the truth of Zen through the instruction of a good master, I said, 'mountains are not mountains, waters are not waters.' But now, having attained the abode of final rest, I say, 'mountains are really mountains, waters are really waters.'

Alienation gives way to the perspective of Suchness in things as the illusions that they are, rather than putting labels on them. Giving the world its right and its power to show itself on its own terms means understanding. Simplicity of mind opens the door to the inner peace of being.

To speak as non-personal singularities, as infinitives, to paraphrase from the Upanishads which says that the self is pure awareness, shines as the light within the heart, surrounded by the senses. Only seeming to think, seeming to move, the Self neither sleeps nor wakes nor dreams. Night and day are brought to fall. A wise goddess riding out of night on the mare of wisdom holding a beacon of light. Maiden beguiled by her soft words brought to the world the hope of a new light, the wisdom of truth. Not with elemental fashion of this or that passing fad, the light that is squelched by water.

Being water. Sliding to the low places. Acting in humility. Embracing selflessness. The more one withdrawals from suffering, the more abundance flows in, the more selfless one becomes, the more one has, and this is the paradox. Logically it does not make sense that more detached the more connected the mind becomes to the cosmic field that resonates pure love. Our underlying substance of connection, the cosmic field, may serve as a recording machine documenting everything, every thought, every emotion, and therefore whatever the subject puts out, is recorded in the cosmic field and comes back to it, sometimes several folds more. Intentions behind the mask of the self, become what the self is. Output is what is attracted towards the self. Self attracts self. Therefore, the boundless open sea is the Ocean of the cosmic field. Mind-tribes outwardly resonate the energy that is already within the subject. Beneath all the hatred, the animosity, anger, and anxiety, there is Love, a resonance so strong that it can permeate through the antagonisms in the material-mask worn by the ego-in-the-world.

Notice the asymmetrical nature of existence but let not these little wars in the world become part of the self and its inner essence. Wardens of earth keep us strapped to the unevenness of temporal causes. Meditation tries to overcome in the singular repetition of the mantra – "OM", which it is believed brings the mind in tune with the natural rhythms of the universe.

While there are atheists who are Buddhists and do not believe in God, the distinction is that in Buddhism there is usually some semblance of transcendence, as the will to overcome an untrained mind.

Love, Joy, and Happiness, overcome all socially constructed antagonisms through meditative practice. Whether we are free is one question but how can we really KNOW we are free unless we first imagine what it MEANS to be free. Simply put, no other definition of freedom is necessary besides knowing that freedom entails a life lived Joyfully. As my variation on a famous saying goes: Truth, Freedom, and Crab Soup, those are the things that matter most to people. Everyone seeks a life based on Truth, Freedom, and (fill in the blank however you will) the third concept is yours to discover for yourself and it illuminates the terms and conditions of the previous two concepts in your own personal subjective way. For some it may be Truth, Freedom, spending time fly fishing. For others it may be Truth, Freedom, and writing poetry. For someone else it may be Truth, Freedom, serving the community through the best of your abilities as a physician, being a responsible parent, being a friend to someone who needs it, and greatest gift in life is that you can find out for yourself what that third term is for you.

Notably, Buddhism's immanent dimensions are at odds with the typical Western Judeo-Christian-Islamic Religions, whereby notable Buddhist philosopher Nishitani Keiji vowed to bring together the Buddha's "Vow of Compassion" as the name for the unity of the Buddha and all things. In contrast with Western religions, Buddhism did not come into existence by proclaiming certain historical facts to be the foundation of its faith. Buddhism arose out of the Buddha's realization of the true path to enlightenment and from the attempt to bear testimony through the practice of the dharma.

Someone more famous than me who academics will say lends my writing 'credibility' once said: Truth is an illusion we have forgotten is such.

As well-worn coins completely effaced to be little more than metal tokens containing no a-priori value. Deconstruction is the open-denouement of nihilism. Nothingness, which is the underlying paradox of being, that it appears to be something, when it is a not (rather, it is a nothing that noths. There are even men, whose social reality is uniquely that of the Not, who will live and die, having forever been only a Not upon the earth. A negation of a negation rather than a positive affirmation, and Sartre claimed that the people whose sole purpose was to be the Not, were caretakers, nurses, and public servants in positions where they see suffering daily. As the first of the four noble truths tell us: there is suffering. Acknowledging that it is there is the first step in overcoming it, but also realizing that it will never go away, until the self is completely negated is to find the truth of Sunyata or emptiness. Because these people are 'taught' at colleges these philosophers somehow lend credibility to my opinions – but, I will not cite anyone. No one reads academic journals. No one reads (period, end of sentence).

Absolute nothingness takes on significance as it actively moves the subject and animates it as its trained intentions begin a new life. In Mahayana Buddhism, this would be the "marvelous being" aspect of the key phrase, true emptiness, marvelous being.

The differences between East and West are becoming evermore elided in the homogenization of culture. The Ocean that takes in all the million little droplets, and makes the divisions into Oneness through the hyper-systematization of life is a real threat to singularity. Tuning out and dropping out of the mainstream culture are survival skills. Lines of flight are meditation practices whereby the dispersion of consciousness, the de-assemblage of the mind into factions can be a necessary tool to see the component parts, the gestalt, the partial objects, that create the possibility of shooting off and creating a counter-hegemonic bloc, an underground. Buddhism is this process. By sitting and silently listening to the mind the subject befriends itself, and disambiguates/extirpates its singularity from the Ocean. Meditation can rekindle a sense of preservation and worth that is far more valuable than the acquired tokens of consumerism that capitalism can offer as trophies to the select few. For Buddhism, consciousness, like every other phenomenon (dharma) is empty (sunyata). To be is to live within conditions, to be conditioned, and to respond to this circumstance as an immediate reflux.

You are what your deep driving desire is. As your desire is, so is your will. As your will is, so is your deed. As your deed is, so is your destiny.

WHEN ALL THE desires that surge in the heart are renounced, the mortal becomes immortal, when all the knots that strangle the heart are loosened, the mortal becomes immortal, here in this very life.

THE KNOTS IN desire can be untied through the practice of meditation. Storing up too much trivial junk in the mind happens to bog it down, and knowledge can be circular in nature. What the Upanishads teaches is wisdom, the timeless beliefs that instill the art of living in the subject, something that is sorely lacking in contemporary society, which has lost its bearings in cultural excess and wanton pleasure seeking. The morass of desires in the marketplace is confounding to the subject that seeks enlightenment through simplicity. Meditation offers a stripping down of the mind to its core functions. When it is stripped to a minimalist state then it can truly focus on what lays before it. The goal being to detach from the tyranny of the past (regret), and the tyranny of the future (anxiety and worry).

Existence is not a problem. The immediacy of being reveals itself in non-problematic terms to the pure intellect. Existence, as such, does not demand definition. A frenetic pace of constant and perpetual becoming can be dizzying, which is why there is also a centrifugal core to the self, beyond the metaphysical movements of the material/physical realm (i.e. the realm of nature and objects). Most world religions call this a soul, but in Buddhist ontology, the desire to know thyself is constantly up for grabs. Once a stable self appears, it is to be deconstructed and ultimately surpassed. Even the Buddha is an object towards which detachment is practiced. As the famous Buddhist saying goes, "If the Buddha crosses your path, kill him!"

# Simply Zen

TRUTH DOES NOT MOVE IN A STRAIGHT LINE. TRUTH IS AN ARC. So is history. So is progress. The arc of history bends towards happiness, but not in the ways one might predict. Waves crashing into the eroding rocks on a distant shore. Times when the currents of truth crest into high tide and fallow periods of winnowing into a low tide the sands of times are exposed. Let us think progress and becoming. Both are constructed as action/thoughts-moving-into-future. Truth in the past may have had mathematical connotations that appear as the linear progression of progress as a clear path directly from one point to another point. No readymade clear-cut paths that lead through the golden road to truth exist. If ever there will be a clear path, one must do the cutting, slashing, clearing, and create the path. If there is a path it will inevitably become a lonely and quiet path that one travels in solitude. Venturing out into the thicket one may find oneself and one may lose oneself. But this is a euro-centric view of writing and epistemology. The word 'wen' in Chinese means many more things than simply writing:

> "It signifies a conglomeration of marks, the simple symbol
> in writing. It applies to the veins in stones and wood, to con-
> stellations, represented by the stokes connecting the stars, to

the tracks of birds and quadrupeds on the ground (Chinese tradition would have it that the observation of these tracks suggested the invention of writing), to tattoo and even for example, to the designs that decorate the turtle's shell ("The turtle is wise," an ancient texts says – gifted with magico-religious powers – "for it carries designs on its back"). The term wen has designated, by extension, literature and social courtesy. Its antonyms are the words wu (warrior, military) and zhi (brute matter not yet polished or ornamented)." (Derrida, 123-4)

Is it getting better, every day, in every way? Does the passage of time imply progress occurs? Every day in every way things were getting better and better? Seems to summarize a predominant myth. Time as a progressive measure of history seems an outdated understanding of history. Unless you create a new way of understanding time as a squiggly line drawn forward, then setbacks, pitfalls, curvatures, struggles to climb back to level ground, movement measured in inches, and then broad expanses where the subject of history can see vast areas of land beyond the horizon, crystal lucid thinking that propels cogent action, and sometimes ethics means moving completely off the grid as if to fly like Yeats' falcon that can no longer hear its falconer. To exist external to the circle of time means that being still relates to the circle in being external to it.

Winds of change seem to sweep over each new day as the deputies of the dominant culture bring gifts to us in the form of the headline of the day. Is it polite to refuse an unwanted gift? Sometimes a gift tells us more about the giver than the intended recipient. Headlines are supposed to give audiences a feeling of being informed about the world. Usually, they tell us nothing objectively true about the world other than what television producers have figured will get ratings and keep eyeballs glued to the sets through commercial breaks so they can sell advertising time to sponsors. Beware the subtle winds of superficiality, gust and blow, be like the willow tree, bend without breaking, be limber, and find strength in bending without breaking in the wind. Who has become the God of Winds? Who informs the opinions of our daily lives? New technologies create new technologies of self that can dismantle any sense of formidable resistance.

Conserve and withdrawal. A healthy sense of cynicism is fine a healthy sense of 'truth as an illusion we have forgotten is an illusion' is much better. Remember that politics is a game that is made up, that economies are games that are made up, that these systems of power are fragile and are most often based on a precipice of manipulating emotions (guilt, shame, fear, enthusiasm, hope, comic relief, and not the deeper channels of Joy revealed to us in the previous chapters). News can be a tool to navigate awkward social interactions on a superficial level. To make small talk with people in forced social situations, around the water cooler, at family gatherings, holidays, so forth, but it does not actually inform anyone of anything other than placate superficial needs to have our image of ourselves as 'intelligent'-'informed'-ego-beings mirrored back to us, so as to sell us toothpaste, insurance, cars, fashions, all the necessary consumer trappings that go along with the underlying insecurities that these feelings mask.

We as humans are tool making animals. A tool is different from a piece of technology. Tools are used to transform the realm of actual material. Technology implies some level of automation that functions in virtual space. Manual labor is supplemented by tools. Technology is often used to gather and then disseminate information and data on the level of virtual space. Music held on an Mp3 player exists to be disseminated through technology. A hammer and nails are tools that manual laborers use to construct physical actual homes. Disconnect between people who live lives in the virtual space of technology. Whose jobs center around those kinds of gadgets and who hover around screens for information and those whose liveliness center around tools. Mechanics working on cars. Carpenters who fix and build homes. Plumbers who unclog leaky drains. Electricians who work on the circuitry and wiring in homes that bring us electricity. Before perhaps twenty or thirty years ago, these manual labor jobs that utilized tools were the epitome of high modernism. Now, things have spiraled out of control in the direction of Science, Technology, Engineering, and Math as skills that are allegedly necessary in abundance. Because of the over-technification of modernity, attention spans are less than they ever were before. Reading a book like this may seem daunting to some because a glut of information, trivia, and data allows people to feel informed in such a way so as to avoid penetrating self-observation and observations offered by 'Others' – usually, bringing the self into existence through observation brings  sorrow. It is not my intention to be the bearer of bad news, but please do not kill the weatherman who honestly reports it will rain tomorrow and then act disappointed with the storm that happens the very next day.

NEGATIVE LIFE EVENTS + exacerbated by a personal inferential style = depression.

Very little can shield you from negative life events. Personal inferential style may be a matter of choice but whether your personality is nature or nurture it does not matter, either way, you were programmed. The honest mistake people make is thinking they are in control when they are not in control of their lives. Automatic responses and stream of consciousness are the modus operandi of the vast majority of 'humans' on this planet, yet, this might also describe a machine that is spitting back information feed into a database. A search engine may give a more deeply thought out automatic response with more empathy about the person doing the search than the actual person who is typing in the words. A computer may store data on the person's search history, purchasing patterns, and befriend that person in ways human beings may not, by remembering that data and presenting it to the person by offering helpful suggestions on gift items, valuable dates to remember, events happening in the person's area, upcoming activities the person may be interested in. Having an automatic response that is programmed, either by nature of nurture does not make the person a person, computers can do these sorts of things quicker than humans can. Unexpectedly responding with creativity in a non-patterned improvisational way that expresses singularity – THAT is what differentiates a human from a computer – that is what you might call intelligence. Intelligence can occur through careful mining of thought in its bare essence in silence – silence gives the mind a clearing with which it can hear itself think.

WHAT IS A FIT of narcissistic rage? Occurs when the expectation that the world will supply unconditional affection is not met. When that 'gleam in the other's eye' known as mirroring fails to approve, confirm, and reward the self sometimes people are let down and you have narcissistic rage. When a culture saturates its people with loving faces that bombard citizens with this nonsense that amounts to massive propaganda designed to sell us 'stuff' the expectation level of unconditional love in our everyday lives may create a threshold greater than what is reasonable to expect from ordinary human beings with pressures and stresses of their own to deal with, let alone when catastrophes strike. Is the rest of the world supposed to change? Asking this is completely narcissistic of course. Selves construct meaning from the tools of language and activity. Language puts contexts and signifiers on experience which may be communicated through memory and/or projections of oneself into the future.

At best these tools give us a superficial depiction of reality and ourselves.

At worst, these serve as complete distortions.

Human consciousness, little more than a bundle of habits, experiences, memories, that form a basis for the trances people live. We are spiders spinning webs. Webs spun to create a self and a spider creates a web without asking why – it simply knows it must create the web. A song on the radio can bring back a memory that conjures up old emotions, old traumas, and old habits.

Big Bopper used to remind my parents of the hamburger stand and lovers lane. Once the subject is aware that this is happening, liberation involves the conscious drive to limit the oppressive violence that can occur from being mesmerized by these trances. The mind is a terrible master, but a wonderful servant.

# A Circle of Time
## Gratitude for Collective Existence

OUR EXPERIENCE OF TIME TELLS US THAT THERE ARE NO ROUND trips in time. Time may be circular, but it is the high arch, cresting and then falling that we see. Most of the time, time is concealed, and we may have an inkling that time has more elements than what is immediately available to our senses. The other side of the arch is always obscured until it loops back around to where we already stand, our currently held ground. Lost time cannot be found again. Once time is gone time is gone. Time yet to come has yet to arrive and therefore has yet to be greeted.

Gift givers and the present are to be greeted with hospitality. It is only a matter of having polite manners. Money comes and goes and the circulation of money leaves an infinite trace of debt on the body politic. Money comes and goes, here one day, gone tomorrow. Money is a poor lover that lacks commitment. Time contains vast value as the original source of the precious garland. Karma is the round trip on the circle of time going around like spokes on a wheel, the center being empty in the wheel of life. Can you have a memory of something you never experienced? More importantly, if you live long enough as you age indeed you observe the same historical and behavioral life-cycles repeat over and over again. People say the same stupid things. Do the same stupid things. Behave the same stupid ways. Get themselves caught in the same moral-traps.

At a certain point, the whole experience of being alive begins to bore you. It is not new anymore and once that new-car-smell wears off, life simply becomes a matter of boring shitty drudge work that just drags on and on and on day in and day out. In youth, life seems to be a sort of theatrical stage play and you are waiting in the audience anticipating the raising of the curtain. Then, adulthood hits you like a ton of bricks, but not instantaneously, a ton of bricks that gradually hits you over the course of a decade, perhaps several decades.

You move to the other side of the curtain and find out that the stage play you were eagerly anticipating is merely the play of shadows bouncing off a cave wall with light reflected from behind you as you are shackled in place. It is all a sham and usually not worth the price of admission to the show. People learn the same clichés from these horrifically dull shadow plays, these shadows have an enormous, and perhaps irreparable impact on the course of human behavior. Life can only be understood backwards, but it must be lived forwards as Soren Kierkegaard once said.

When I was a child my grandmother painted a portrait of my brother and I playing with sand on the beach near her cottage in Florida. When we celebrated the first birthday party for my daughter Ava there was a snapshot taken of her in my arms wading ankle deep in a shallow pond in Windsor, New York near where we lived at the time. These two images mirrored each other so closely that they may represent a circular sense of temporality, that is, a memory that circulated back to me through time from the past into that present moment. In recollecting the picture with my daughter, I often describe it to my wife as precisely the happiest moment of my life. It may have been because it resonated with the deep seated subconscious memory of a younger me playing on the beach. Since the picture with my daughter is cloudy it gives off the impression that it is taking place in heaven. Capturing the exact feeling of bliss that I experienced.

As with so many beautiful fleeting brushes with the mystical perhaps it occurred to me only in hindsight that I had momentarily transcended into heaven. It may be sad to ponder such unreasonable expectations of life that occur in hindsight to be empty promises never to be kept with myself – at the time of my daughter turning one-year old I was a mover and shaker on the make in graduate school. Working on a doctoral degree gave me the impression that something big was just around the corner. Greatness was so close I could feel it and I had been bristling with enthusiasm for so long that the excitement became a normal part of life as typical emotional wallpaper to my everyday emotions. Surely, I am not alone in thinking that adulthood would have great things in store. Most people have to carry in themselves some sense of importance in order to put up with all the humiliating nonsense that goes into existing in modern life. Wishing that things might be better, if you simply hang in there, like that cliché cat poster hanging on so many bulletin boards in cubicle spaces.

Now, looking back, those things were foolish. The experiences I yearned for, were already there in the love of the people who surrounded me. It is sad to think that all we remember now that is gone was once there so vivid, brushing by, like strangers whisking away to this or that important thing, millions of people zipping along in cities around the world, never speaking, never stopping to meet and greet, so important at that time. Now, I realize it will no longer be there. All those people will pass. All those 'things' all that 'stuff' that seemed so crucial at that time will melt into the void. It is almost as if the zipping by resembles the void already; we are already IN the void by the lack of meaningful connections we attend to while being-here.

Time is fleeting and yet the sense that we have of time is precisely the sense of being with which we greet the gift of the present. Welcoming the present and entering each moment as if it were a beautiful gift from a warm endearing friend may transform all the memories leading up to that moment, as if, there was some fate along the way leading to this 'satori' moment (satori being the Japanese term for instant enlightenment).

Falling out of time and being 'beside oneself' in time and in relations to others as they traverse time in their own sense of living their time, is precisely the technical sense of 'paranoia' – a sense of being beside oneself, self-alienated, or dualistically relating one warring faction of the self to another warring faction. Paranoia may be nothing more than a subconscious tactical correction in the imagination meant to adapt consciousness to a disturbance in Ultimate Reality.

Becoming whole by reflecting on which aspects of the self, polarities coming back around into unity, spatial and temporal boomeranging of the self. The story of how I began meditating seriously was this exact phenomenon – I quit adjunct teaching after several years of commanding zero respect, my wife, kids and I picked up and moved to Lewiston, New York. Where I took a modest income working as a scholarly editor at an out of the way academic press with little or no notoriety except of possibly negative connotations in the academic field. I wanted to take a break from the peanuts pay of teaching.

Day after day, I pored over manuscripts in this sort cul-de-sac editing job, every day I walked out of work, stressed, gaining weight, sad, depressed, on prescription mood stabilizers, unhealthy, angry, unfulfilled. One day, I looked up, and saw a window across the street from my job, with statues of the Buddha and a beautiful lotus garden. It said, "Blue Lotus Zen Center"; there was a phone number. I called and left a message. Made an appointment with a man named Wei-Bo, who greeted me a few days later. We talked, and it was as if the 'universe' or 'God' or whatever you might call it, put this doorway so close, made the path so easy, so obvious that it would be unavoidable for me to miss the clues. Yet, it was fully up to me to take the time to walk through those doors. The doors of perception that would forever change my life. Every Sunday for three years I meditated in the morning. Came home to a loud noisy home, went to an unfulfilling job at the editing company, and then took a leap to take a minimum wage job in vitamin sales, and go back into adjunct teaching. This time, knowing more about the cul-de-sac of private enterprise.

Scenes like the ones just describe typify a retrospectively oriented phenomenon of a very personal memory of an experience in my life related to my perception of time. Even in our everyday lives we are challenged daily to think an ontology that presumes that in making there is doing and in doing there is justification for our existence. To think a communist ontology that is something other than a merely equal distribution. To settle for a thought of justice as simply a fair piece of the pie is to invalidate the revolutionary possibilities of this novel ontology.

In other words, Nishida's novel ontology is not a thought of distributive justice, in the sense of equally divvying up scarce commodities for consumption. It is rather a thought of the common of experiences that are not based on a metaphysic of value. A share of the whole in common experiences such as language, space, and time. What are we to think of time and when time runs out in death? If when we pass there is a crossing over to the afterlife then should we be scared? Think of it this way we can be reunited with lost loved ones. We can also have the luxury of conversing with anyone from history. Discussing philosophy with Friedrich Nietzsche himself would be an honor – or, Homer, Descartes, the Buddha, Jesus, and see Jimi Hendrix cut an album with Ludwig von Beethoven and Kurt Cobain. Certainly, would be a hard rocking album!

If there is nothing and our consciousness does not transcend into a crossing over then, there is nothing to worry about because we may not feel, see, hear, smell, or taste anything at that point, unless our sense of perception transcends the death of our physical bodies. Timelessness in eternity without any sense perception and therefore "void" of any consciousness means that the "I" would cease to exist and a huge sigh of relief would occur – nothing there to feel pain or to even be self-aware enough to exist as consciousness. I think therefore I am means that ceasing to think means one ceases to exist. Eternal void makes thought impossible.

THE COMMON CONCEPTION of time is that it progresses in a linear fashion like a straight line. This conception of time is flawed because it lacks an ontological understanding of how time is experienced. Understanding time as linear also creates a faulty understanding of how historical epochs progress by assuming each successive epoch is akin to the linear progression of directly from the previous epoch.

It is like construing history as an organism that is growing more and more complex where the previous instant is thought to have vanished forever, never to be recollected at a future time. What is intriguing about Nishida's ontology is that the trace of the past is always immanent within the being's comportment, or movement toward the present. This relation to the present ultimately influences the being's anticipation of the future.

Experience is historical rather than universal to everyone. It is inextricably bound to the contingency of what has occurred and the possibility of what may become. The past, although only understood through memory may become distorted, it is never absent it is a factory producing the present. Time must, in one aspect, be circular. But to say that time is circular, linking past and future, is to negate time. Or to think of time as an existential contradiction. To think of the past as not yet passed, or the future, although not yet come, as already appearing. This is the challenge before us here today. To think time as a future that is heralded now. The future has a shadow cast over the here and now. If one thinks of the past and future as linked, in one large coterminous circle, then this is a radically different conception of time than we are used to in Western ontology.

IF TIME IS circular, what kind of circle is it? For some it may be a gentle swirling flow as in a lovely humming whirlpool one relaxes in at the end of a hard day of work. For others it may be the whizzing and whirring of a violent tornado that sucks up and destroys everything in its path. Or, wasted time may simply expunge the circular flow of water, life as nothing more than flushing refuse down a dingy toilet.

It is a thought of the permanent instant that is constantly changing, swirling, flowing, moving, and yet a stasis in the middle, peace at the center. In this sense, it is possible to think of time as the erasure of the instant, or as the instant as nothing more than a series of now, now, nows. Can we create a name for every leaf at every moment? Thinking of a series of instants is not necessarily the same as thinking a novel characterization of beings at each moment.

You are not completely different from one instant to the next. Some of the self remains from the previous moment and so there is a bit of you that continuously remains the same from one instant to the next, even though, paradoxically, there is no stable "I". At the same time, there is something that is different. As some instant passes, you are a bit older and a bit closer to death so you have changed in that regard. In this sense, there is a bit of you that is discontinuous from yourself in the previous moment.

Slip sliding away at every moment of the day. What remains true in both instances is that there is no singular property that makes up a given essence of the person from instant to instant. There are characteristics that remain from the previous instant into future instants and there are new characteristics that change yet there is no one property that remains obstinate from moment to moment that constitutes the individual's own-most identity. This perception of identity shifts as temporality fluctuates and changes over the course of the passage of time.

So, Nishida thinks a different, circular conception of time, not as a measure but a thought of the instant as a pure abstraction in the sense that if you cannot think the instant you cannot think time. Time is not necessarily made of a continuous series of instants linked together in a linear fashion. These instants are continuous and discontinuous, which is a contradiction people must be willing to live with if they are to understand the true nature of time and existence. Can you touch time? Is an instant graspable? Of course, this is absurd to think this way. The before and after that is represented in time are always linked therefore it is impossible to conceive of time without conceptualizing it as an instant.

Now is always now, yet now is distinctly different from then even though there would be no now without a becoming out of the only then that occurred. Recollection of the past is always an anticipation of the future and vice versa. In this sense time is always based on a circular experience. There can be no now without a then having occurred and there can be no future without our anticipation of it having already shaped the future from the beginning. One must have a recollection to provide the perspective on which to base an anticipation of the future. Recollection and anticipation are always packaged together giving a circular nature to this novel ontology.

The circular nature of time does not forestall the possibility of revolution, but presages a revolution that will interrupt the future through the co-immanence of poiesis and being. The tools utilized in the production process determine to large extent the consciousness of general intellect that is associated with the possibility of revolutionary subject. The circular nature of time is a contradiction to be dealt with, not overlooked, however the poiesis of production itself is where the truly revolutionary possibilities exist. New waves of technology designed to reduce the production process to zero and designed to increase productivity to an infinite speed are always reshaping the way the worker is subsumed within the production process.

The essential component of production is the worker's relation to the tool in which the worker becomes the prosthesis to production. Subjection is propertylessness. In the sense that the worker has been excluded from property ownership, but also in the sense that the worker's essence is always wrapped up in relation to the mechanization of the production process. The real virtuoso of production is that which can perform all of the tasks necessary to complete the production process. A virtuoso cannot the worker, but the machine itself. The worker is ultimately an appendage to the causa sui of the machines. That is, the cause that has no cause. Is God a cause that has no cause? A cause that caused itself? In modern capitalism – the creative-being previously understood to be "God" was replaced by the machine and the human creativity that caused machinic production. Human intellect was the key to the creative powers of production.

Creative process is like an architect that plans a blueprint before constructing a building. Bees do not do this when creating their hives. Spiders do not do this when spinning their webs. Humans can do this if we plan and remain some sense of patience in understanding where we want to go. Building and planning towards fully automated mechanized production. Basho, or place, indicates that what we call operations of consciousness cannot be isolated from the world; to the extent that it be thought to be existing. Consciousness must first be the temporal aspect of the temporal spatial world. Consciousness cannot be conscious of consciousness. Consciousness first mirrors what is around consciousness. Patience, quiet, humility, and meditation are the ingredients in the recipe for consciousness.

This is a circularity based on individual perceptions of time, not be confused with the common notion of history as a banal repetition of itself. This circular ontology is not the repetition of historical epochs, but a projection of past experiences into the future. A unity of time in the sense that we can produce and communicating through a common language about time.

WHAT IS AT stake is a thought of futurity informed by possibility that instants are radically discontinuous while remaining continuous simultaneously. Continuous discontinuity is another willing-ingredient in the recipe for consciousness. Breaking old habits (the way the world 'naturally' produces sickness) to create new habits (seeing the world afresh). Willing to dismantle the trances that created 'you' before 'you' were old enough to truly know you were being constructed by external forces. To distill the voices of relatives in the mind, the voices of numerous Others that clutter the mind. Tribes of people live in each mind, it takes a lifetime to narrow down the mind to a village containing only yourself.

To think of future revolutions as an overcoming or absolute rupture with the past is to remain naïve about the contradictions inherent in understanding time. Similitude between what mediates and what is mediated is a thought that mediation is the only possibility insofar as what has happened is happening. Space belongs to time in the sense that the spatializing of time is always linked to the temporalization of space, regardless of what Heidegger said on this topic. Existence is the only limitation on what is possible yet everywhere we look there are promises that everything is possible at all moments. Possibility is a package deal with marketing, "Everything is possible with the right car!"

Impossible is only possible in the realm of the imaginary. Yet this sort of revolutionary subjectivity pulls the rug out from underneath developmental models of revolution and human consciousness.

THE CONCEPT OF facticity implies that an entity within-the-world has Being-in-the-World in such a way that it can understand itself as bound up in its destiny with the being of those entities which it encounters within its own world. Time and Being is the exact text where Heidegger hinted at this inverted conception of time. For time = a nothing spatialized. I did not want to say there that time 'is' a nothing spatialized, because that would mean that time is a being and that would mean time would be defined as a something-spatialized. A sentence like that would implode on itself. Calming the waters in the pool of the mind and then space and time settle in their emergence as the silent essence of "it" emerge. "It" that emerges is the pervasive force shaping our understanding of being. Implacable. Unnamable. Making declarative statements (such as these) about time is impossible - "it" is not an object to be possessed.

When Plato represents Being as idea, and as the koinonia of the Ideas, when Aristotle represents it as energeia, Kant as position, Hegel as the absolute concept, Nietzsche as the will to power.

Words of Being as answers to a claim which speaks in the sending, concealing in the "there is, it gives, Being."

Always retained in the withdrawing, sending, being is unconcealed for thinking with its epochal abundance of transmutations emerging in silent stillness ... (_____) form is void.

Being... "it" gives... a new meaning, a new conception of what is understood as truth and existence. Il Ya... it gives. Being is a gift, a new event, giving a new meaning to an occurrence which previously held no language to describe it. Inventing a signifier because the sign it represents did not exist previously.

Giving showed itself as sending. A message sent out to the rest of the world, only to gain currency as it was circulated and deemed to be a relevant estimation of an actual event. Existence always precedes essence in this case.

IN HIS LECTURE *Time and Being*, Martin Heidegger assumes a linear conception of time in which existence is the precedent for essence. There is, it gives, Being. Waiting for Godot, "If I hang myself will I have an orgasm?" How far towards death do we have to drift before an event will occur? Being brings into existence new beings which depend upon Being to be created at all. Being is the spirit behind existence that is creation, but it is also a thought of now. Difference is never overcome in the One and the One is never anything than its articulation in difference from itself. In taking a cue from Descartes, the Cogito did not go far enough with reflection. If doubt is the basis of thought and all inquiry into the nature of reality begins with pondering whether it exists, then taking this process to its fulfillment would ultimately lead to radical skepticism about the existence of the Self.

Money cannot buy more time. Once time is gone its gone. If I had one wish it would be have more time in life. Now, try to understand me. I DO NOT want immortality. That is a horrifying bridge too far never dying would probably be more terrifying than having never been born at all.

No...

I want the time of an Old Testament Protagonist, a Moses, an Abraham, a Noah.

The mythologies of the Old Testament are completely harmonious with my utopian idea of what a perfect lifespan should be, something like a slothful 700-900 years, loafing around, having enough time to get tons of shit done, close readings of all the books on my bucket list, travelling, planning out life decisions, Not this bullshit we are stuck with now of scrambling around in a mere 70, 80, maybe 90 years working to survive and basically winding up dead by the time you blink. Bluster of smoke, mirrors, sound, fury, and then poof...it's gone! It would be nice to think about that and to imagine what could be done with all that time coupled with some urgency in knowing the time still ends someday, like the veil of the apocalypse that hangs over some Christian-believers. Coating the suffering in the violent hope that God will someday soon wipe life completely off the face of the earth. How optimistic! How sick to think of the greatest gift as a disease to be cured?

I MEAN, WHAT IS WORK? I'll ruin the surprise - work consists of bribing you to speed up your death by selling your time in weekly installment plans. Work means forfeiting your time until you die...so on so forth. Its forced socialization, usually with sociopaths.

The psychotic notion that your thoughts influence the external world is nothing more than what is the case, your dreams seem possible because dreams are possible. Stop dreaming you are alive because you are. You are alive because you can still dream. You are not a narrow idiot that is why I kept this book purposefully opaque and you made it all the way to the end. Congratulations!

Memories of dream makers resting outside of the universe. What a bizarre thought that brings much paranoia – unless we are already unified with these dream makers. Unless we make our own dreams. Unless we have nothing to worry about because we are always already raindrops flowing within the boundless open sea!

www.ingramcontent.com/pod-product-compliance
Lightning Source LLC
Chambersburg PA
CBHW052108090426
42741CB00009B/1718